To Lawrence .

Nik Coppin's
Comedy World
By
Nik Coppin

Edited by Stuart Reid

Cover art and design by John Pender and Stuart Reid

Illustrations by Nik Coppin

Keep Supporting
Live Comedy!
Love and hugs,
Nik Coppin.

Gorgeous Garage Publishing Ltd
Scotland

Cover design by John Pender
Cover copyright ©Gorgeous Garage Publishing Ltd
Illustrations by Nik Coppin copyright ©Nik Coppin
Back cover photograph by Mike Lebowski

Photographs used by kind permission of Nik Coppin

All quotes used with the kind permission of
'Fat' Freddy Morris, Ciara Donaldson and Andrew Roper
Foreword by Henning Wehn

This first edition published in the UK
by Gorgeous Garage Publishing Ltd

ISBN : 978-1-910614-14-3

http://www.nikcoppin.com

DEDICATION

For my Mum and Dad
Because let's face, I wouldn't be here with out them.

Both funny in their own ways.
And well, you know, because I love them of course.

CONTENTS

"I highly recommend getting your hands on a copy this book. It's a great laugh... and if we go into lockdown again you may need more toilet paper!"
Andrew Roper - "Legendary" Australian Comedian

Henning Wehn
German Comedy Ambassador to the United Kingdom

Foreword by Henning Wehn

Dear Readers,

I never expected for it to come to this: being asked to jot down a few words for a book written and illustrated by Nicholas Odie Coppin.

Nik's my best mate in comedy and he was one of the first people I met on the circuit all the way back in the early noughties, by which time Nik was already established. Some acts have five year plans, Nik has a 50 year plan and it's on track.

As he doesn't tire of saying: "Anything is better than being back on the Underground", where he worked for 15 years and when you hear stories of him playing football in the signal cabin or almost electrocuting a maintenance crew by mistakenly making the tracks live, Transport for London might be saying much the same.

This book is a great insight into life on the road. Europe, Asia, Australia – Coppin knows his way around. Few people have travelled the comedy world more extensively than the man inexplicably dressed like an 8-year old: in Spider-Man t-shirt and baseball cap.

We all know he can talk for England and Barbados but this book also shows one of his other talents: he's a great illustrator! He also has a great range of accents but they're notoriously difficult to showcase in a book.

Please enjoy some of the many, many stories from the complete one-off that is Nicholas Odie Coppin! It's a privilege to have played a small part in some of them.

On to the Second Volume!

Henning

Introduction

People often ask what it's like doing stand-up comedy, how one got into it, why one does it and all of that business.

But rather than talk about those whys and wherefores, more interesting would be the deep-down psychological and emotional reasons that myself and many fellow comedians do such a job, or have such a vocation rather.

These things should really be discussed in my inaugural comedy book.

To gaze into a comedian's psyche and perhaps one's very soul... to dredge those innermost thoughts, fears and insecurities that make us travel the length and breadth of the country, and in some cases the world with the intention of entertaining rooms full of strangers. To assist them in letting go of whatever baggage they may be carrying from weeks and perhaps months of hard work and whatever pain they are feeling and possibly suffering from in their private lives.

Together we can hopefully laugh through the traumas that we all experience. Laughter after all, as many people will tell you, is the best medicine. Surely that would be a marvellous thing to explore in my first book? Surely.

But then I thought, "Fuck that shit man, let's just tell a few anecdotes of my time in the world of comedy and draw some cartoons to go with them."

And of course, after that global pandemic stuff and the 'new normal' world that we now live in, the decision was taken to get this book of shaggy-dog stories out ahead of its planned release date.

As such, I hope you enjoy this exclusive first edition of what is essentially a bit of a rough diamond to get this book into your hands quickly.
If it can take your mind off the current situation, if only for a short while, job done!

Nik x

P.S. I was planning not to have to mention my middle name, so thanks Henning! Yes, Mum named me after American war-hero-turned-actor 'Audie' Murphy. Superstar!

Chapter 1 - The Comedy House

What better place to start than a house full of comedians? Surely a barrel of laughs, right? Wrong.

Don't misunderstand me, the guys I was living with were all jolly good people, just that a house full of professional jesters is not the barrel of laughs that some might think. And it's not like we all got together writing new material and practising it in the living room and stuff.

More often than not, I found myself playing games of chess against the German Comedy Ambassador to the UK in our rather large kitchen area. That's right, Mr Henning Wehn. As hilarious as he can be on and off stage, more serious things like games of chess were the order of the day in the Comedy House.

The 'Comedy House' was a five bedroom place in Crouch End in North London. Or, if you are one of the pretentious middle-class luvvies in the area, 'Croosh Ond'.

It was home to many comedians over the years, and had a reputation for drink and drug fuelled parties. By the time I moved in though, that sort of shit had calmed down, thank God. But we still had more than enough pothead comedians staying over, as well as a couple of very late/early New Year's Eve parties. The last one, I recall the party still going on until about 8am and as such people had commandeered Henning's bedroom, which was on the downstairs floor, so needing sleep, he crawled in beside me in my bed and slept there until early afternoon. How sweet. No sex, just cuddling. Well, maybe just the tip.

I had the good fortune of living in the house with the German Comedy Ambassador, Australian Wayne Deakin who luckily had shed the Chopper Read moustache since I first met him in Melbourne years ago, little Matt Kirshen, a lovely lad with Jewish heritage and Paul Byrne. The latter not being a comedian, but instead a director of shows and brother to comedian Ed Byrne. Good cook too.

Paul moved out after about a year of me being there I believe, then Seymour Mace took his place. Rhyme not intended. Seymour is a north-eastern chap who came to live in London to pick up more gigs down south. However, he spent more of his time on the old wacky baccy than out working, but that suited us lovely, because he would get stoned, bake lots of cakes and fix up the house. Got some great new lino in the toilet, plenty of cupcakes and the occasional Victoria sponge. Yum-yum. Good man.

It should also be noted that the house was situated at the bottom of the infamous street, Cranley Gardens. Those that know their serial killers, will know that at the other end of Cranley Gardens, number 23D, was the flat where Dennis Nilsen lured a number of homeless gay men to, and ultimately their horrific demise, dismemberment and flushing down the bog. To my mind, and rather ironically, both comedians and serial killers are at opposite ends of the same spectrum. What with the kind of madness that goes on in both comedians and serial killers heads, I guess it's just which end of the spectrum they gravitate towards.

Making rooms full of strangers laugh, or removing people's skins and body parts.

We never had any problems with our drains mind. Paying the rent on time, yes, but human body parts in the pipes, never. We often had our landlord, a little Cypriot bloke called Louie chasing us for his money from month-to-month. Odd little chap he was. When you think about it, it is quite amusing having a 4' 11" octogenarian bloke with an accent and all, chasing comedians that are trying to avoid him. He always managed to catch us however. Must've had an eye in the sky.

It wasn't always hiding from the landlord and moving chess pieces around a board though, which was fortunate because Henning always won. I do remember winning one game, but that might have just happened in my noggin. There were obviously some great laughs too. One of the most amusing things that happened was one afternoon when I entered Henning's bedroom.

No, his cock wasn't out, even though I'm sure that would have been quite hilarious, if scary, to see his little bratwurst on display.

The story started a few days previous. I was telling Mr Henning a story about something or other and I used the expression, "He's got tickets on himself". Henning asked me what that meant, so I told him that it was a saying that a good friend of mine in Melbourne, Cath Styles, would often use to describe somebody who is really up themselves and a bit of a narcissist.

He replied that that didn't really work as a sentence. Which is quite hypocritical from a man that is constantly saying "out of a sudden", when what he should be saying, and I've told him time and time again for many years, is "all of a sudden"!

Learn to speak proper English, mein freund!

He was of course in this instance, correct. In itself, the sentence 'he's got tickets on himself' doesn't really work. Still, it means what it means. That somebody likes themselves so much, they would buy tickets to see themselves.

So, I'm sitting in the Ambassadors rather comfortable reclining armchair by his bay windows and he's on the computer doing something or other. He then gets his wallet out and starts to tap credit card numbers into the keyboard. I asked him what he's doing and he informs met that he's on the website for the Times newspaper.

I ask him why he needs his credit card for that and he tells me that apparently they've done an article on one of his shows at Wilton's Music Hall in Whitechapel and there is an accompanying video of him on stage.

Therefore, he needs to check the content of the video to see that there is nothing untoward or wrong with it, but there is a paywall, so in order to view it, he has to cough up £1. Actually, as it happens, with regard to such situations that they have done a piece on you, you can obtain a code from somebody at The Times to bypass said paywall, but apparently that is a lot more hassle and time-consuming.

So rather than go through that rigmarole, the German Comedy Ambassador to the UK chose to pay to watch himself!

A living, breathing example of somebody having tickets on themselves right before my very eyes! Brilliantly ironic, but at least the Ambassador finally understood the saying.

Chapter 2 - Donkey Shotty

You will be pleased to know that Henning doesn't just like to get tickets to watch himself. He doesn't mind obtaining a football ticket or two. And bus tickets to get there. On this occasion, to go see a second division match in southern Spain.

The result in the end was Malaga 0, Almeria 1.

I'm not sure if it was a disappointing performance from the home side, or Almería being technically superior, but either way, Malaga at home were very underwhelming indeed. Not showing any real creativity unlike Almeria's goal about 10 minutes in, which for what you might expect at that level of football, was a joy to watch.

Still, for a tier two game of Spanish football, it was all very entertaining indeed.

And no, he didn't just decide one day to purchase the tickets to go and see a game in Spain from London. We were in Spain already. I would like to think that if the Ambassador did want to do such a thing, he would at least get a flight, rather than a bus, to Malaga. We had just spent the last few days together, along with Matt Price and Stefano Paolini doing some fantastic shows on the Spanish coast.

Matt and Stef had scooted back home on the Friday, whereas myself and Henning stayed until the Sunday. Thing was, we had to spend the best part of an hour and a half to get to Malaga on the bus from Estepona and two hours back again, only to have to get a taxi back to Malaga airport the following morning at 9:45am for a 12:45pm flight back to London Gatwick.

Not the best of logistical planning, especially from what I thought was a stereotypically efficient German mind, but the Ambassador does like a bit of football after all. Him being a footy fan however, did result in probably my best and certainly most eye-opening experience with regards to the 'Beautiful Game' a few years back.

That being at the North London home ground of my beloved Arsenal FC, the Emirates Stadium. And not just the regular everyday seats surrounded by disgruntled fans not happy with the lack of spending and ambition of the board of directors and some poor vision and purchasing decisions from the then manager Arsène Wenger. No, proper corporate hospitality, innit. Henning, being the celeb that he is, had a friend in somebody who owned a corporate box, so invited myself and his manager Ian Wilson along to watch the Gunners play his German team FC Schalke 04 in the group stage of the European Champions League. What a thoroughly decent chap he is, the Ambassador.

I suspected I was at least in for a tip-top view of the match, some free booze and perhaps a nice buffet laid on in the box, but how wrong could I have been? After a few sherbets in a local pub in the Finsbury Park area, we walked to the stadium and then into a room where the first thing I saw was a gargantuan Arsenal crest mounted on a shiny mahogany wall. Almost as big as the audiences on one of the Ambassador's UK tours.

Absolutely beautiful it was.

If that wasn't impressive enough for my already bulging eyes, the mountains of roast beef, salmon and all the vegetables you could eat certainly got them way bigger than my belly. Oh. My. God! Where to start? Roast beef, of course. Followed by salmon, and then maybe some vegetables. Maybe. Let's not go crazy on the vegetables now. Grog too! FREE grog!

Surrounding us and the food of course were a few celebrities too. A conversation with Lofty from EastEnders being a nice little highlight. Then more free booze in the corporate box as we watched Arsenal go down 2-0 to the Germans. The Gooners had a promising opening 10 minutes, then proceeded to be picked apart and made look a bit second rate, for the next 80 minutes. I dread to think what the fans in the 'cheap seats' (anyone who's ever bought a season ticket or even a regular ticket to watch The Arsenal play, will truly understand the irony in that statement) were saying about the board and the management after that one. Myself however, I don't think I've ever felt less disappointed watching Arsenal lose. The beef, salmon, booze, and celebrity-spotting took care of what would have been abject misery for me. And of course, that abundance of free red wine always helps to numb the pain.

Anyway, Spain. So, there we are after our two hour coach journey back to Estepona, walking back up the hill from the beach to our Airbnb apartment and outside a local bar is more Spanish football playing on the box. From the 'EXT' and 'NUM' codes by the score, we deduced that it was Extremadura playing Numancia and Henning makes a comment about the home team, saying that - and I quote from what my ears took in, "That is where Donkey Shotty is from!"

I'm like, "Who?" And The Ambassador repeats, "Donkey Shotty!", and again I enquire as to who the hell he's talking about.

"You must have heard of Donkey Shotty. He is a Spanish legend. There are stories about him jostling with the windmills and all sorts..."

What the hell is he on about?! I'm totally confused and completely baffled with regards to what my crazy German friend is going on about. Racking not just my brains for this character, thinking it must be some Spanish cartoon donkey with a rifle that for some reason likes to do battle with arch enemies in the form of windmills, but also questioning myself as the whether I am hearing this correctly. For starters, aren't windmills way more of a Dutch than Spanish thing anyway?

How can he possibly be talking about a character Donkey Shotty?! So I'm running through it both internally and outwardly over and over again as he repeatedly says, "DONKEY SHOTTY! DONKEY SHOTTY!". Both of us getting louder and louder as I question whether this character exists and him not understanding why I'm not getting who this character is.

So I start to break it down in mind. I'm thinking maybe the first name is 'Don'. But what Don has the surname, 'Keyshotty'?!"

Then all of a sudden, a breakthrough, when the Ambassador says, "Going around with his friend Sancho Panza…" Wait, I know that name!

"You mean DON QUIXOTE!!!!!"

"FOR FUCK SAKE MAN! It's DON QUIXOTE! DON QUIXOTE! Not fucking DONKEY SHOTTY!"

"That's how we say it in Germany. Well, 'Don Keyshot', but in Spain it's 'Don Keyshot-ey." I shout "No, it's not, you dick! It's pronounced Don Kee-ho-tee!"

"Not in Germany".

Blimey O'Reilly! The "out of a sudden" nonsense is bad enough. But now this?! Not only did I think the Ambassador was an intelligent bloke, but proof right there and I rest my case ladies and gentlemen, that the whole world should just speak English and be done with it!

"Let me at those windmills!"

Chapter 3 - Henning and the Leprechaun

I've done a few gigs in the Republic of Ireland and every single one has been in County Cork, for some reason. One of those reasons would be that my friend Mary lives in Churchtown there and has arranged a couple of things in pubs and theatres.

Churchtown being a small Irish village, I guess you would call it, where the late, great Oliver Reed lived prior to his death whilst filming Gladiator in Malta. I actually visited his grave while I was there. Bit grim, but whatever.

Apparently he used to drink in this little local pub where I did a weird gig once, and my friend Mary and some of the locals told me that he would go in the pub and often treat the locals to loads of booze, on account of him being on the rather wealthy side of life.

But then he would get totally lashed out of his head and just start taking the piss out of all the Irish people sat around him. Paying to make fun of people, what an intriguing pastime.

But if the Irish are anything like me and lots of other English people, I'm sure they would happily take copious amounts of free booze from someone who wants to pay for it and then insult you a bit. Bottoms up!

Every gig I have done there seems to work out very strangely indeed, including the one I did in a theatre in Charleville with my comedy matey Mike Belgrave when we were heckled all the way through by a local. It was a fantastically fun show bouncing off this guy in the audience. The timing of his heckles was unbelievably impeccable, which all made sense when we found out after the show that it was a chap by the name of John Kerry, who was quite the celebrity comedian in Ireland, having been part of a famous TV double act.

The weirdest however was years previous to this and again, involved the German Ambassador, Henning Wehn.

The organisation of this gig was such that they were talking about reduced payments or us staying at somebody's house rather than the nice hotel we were promised, resulting in Henning threatening, "Well, I not perform!" if we didn't get all that we were promised. Fair enough, but amusing nonetheless listening to him have a rant in his slightly unusual German cadence.

That in itself wasn't as unusual as the bizarre ritual of mouse racing that was happening in the pub the night before we did the show.

Yes, you read that correctly, mouse racing! I'll try to explain.

In a rather large nutshell, there was this big box with a glass front and eight wooden shelves forming the running lanes inside this box. At one end of the box there were eight rodents in little stalls, much like you would have at the start of a horse race. The gate would open on the stall and off they'd go!

Well, the ones that gave a shit to be involved in this peculiar and outlandish game.

Some of them would stay in their starting area, some weren't even looking in the right direction, others made it about halfway before seemingly getting bored, and one or two actually made it to the other end.

Then the eight mice were encouraged to get back to their stalls for the next race, so another load of people could bet again on the result. After running their little mousey race, a couple of them didn't always want to go back to the start, which meant the old geezer in charge would often have to tip the box up and bang it on the mantelpiece above the fire to shake the the mouse loose and send him tumbling back to his his tiny stall prison, like some kind of Mouschwitz.

The patrons partaking in this ludicrous activity had two options. A straight bet of a euro or two on a chosen mouse, or they could actually bid in an auction to obtain a mouse, in which case they would get a share of that mouse's winnings.

People actually did that too, which was curious given it was the same eight mice every time.

Still, my first race I bet on mouse number six, and I won! I was a few euros to the good, which made me happy and I decided not to bet again to maintain my 100% record! I'm glad I had that victory, especially given that at the show the following night, I died on my fucking arse. I don't think the locals at a pub in Clonakilty, County Cork really took to a gobby mixed-race Englishman.

However, leading up to all of this freakish behaviour, the ever-entertaining, if not always for the right reasons, Comedy Ambassador had us pissing ourselves at Cork International Airport.

En route to Ireland were myself and the German Ambassador obviously, but also good comedy friends by the name of John

Newton and Jem Brookes. For some reason on the Ryanair flight, somebody mentioned the fact that not only will we be partaking in some lovely Guinness, possibly listening to some Irish folk music and seeing the beautiful hills of the Irish landscape, if we are lucky we might also get to see a leprechaun.

Not long being in the UK from Germany, Henning asks the question, "What is a leprechaun?"

Having never actually had to describe a leprechaun to anyone before, I replied, "Well, they are these kind of really small blokes, that live in Ireland. They always have red hair and they wear like, green suits."

Obviously, not the best description, but not bad on the spot.

The Ambassador had an extremely quizzical look on his face and then asks, "Are they real?"

Now, as a Brit talking to a German, I spot an opportunity. One that was not to be missed. So I'm like, "Sure, of course they're real. They live all over Ireland. These little blokes in little green suits and they all have pots of gold."

Henning sensed that I might not be telling the complete truth, so says, "This can't be real," and never one to give up easily on a wind up, I go on, "Why would I lie? Why would I make such a thing up?"

At that, Henning stopped asking questions and appeared to fully take on board everything I've said. Brilliant. At some point he's going to tell people about these leprechauns in Ireland, thinking they are real and going to make a right fool of himself. So internally I am rather pleased with myself about this situation I have potentially created in the future, even though I'm not going to be there.

But, and this is the best bit of the whole trip I reckon, we land at Cork International Airport and as we are getting off the plane, one of the airport staff ushering us towards the terminal - and I shit you not - was a dwarf with ginger hair wearing a bright green luminous jacket!

We could not stop laughing. Especially when Henning went up to him and asked him where his pot of gold was.

I would like to say the story ended there, but given the celebrity Henning was starting become, for years I delighted in telling people that story. Until one day in Edinburgh, a woman from County Cork shouted out, "I know that guy!" "Henning?" I retorted. "No, the little guy!" She said back, "I see him at the airport all the time. His name is Dave!"

Dave the Dwarf? And she knew him! Un-bloody-believable.

Again, never to miss an opportunity, I took everybody's email address in that particular show in the hope that we would all stay in touch for the next time she met Dave and could tell us about it. There were a few emails sent out, but we never did find out if she even encountered Dave and his magical ways.

Sad times, but as the old saying goes, don't sweat the small stuff.

Chapter 4 - Carr Clash

Of course, when you've been in the comedy industry for the best part of twenty years, having done open mic spots to then doing festivals all over the world, you tend to rub shoulders with other big names too. Not just Germanic ones, but of course home-grown too.

One of the more interesting and possibly most confusing encounters I had years ago with a now celebrity, was with one Alan Carr.

For those people that aren't too familiar with the comedy scene, or know about popular TV chat show hosts, I'm talking about the comedian, not the quit smoking bloke.

Yes, the self-styled 'Chatty Man' himself.

To the best of my memory, it would've been in the early 2,000s, or the 'noughties' as I believe they are often known.

I would've been a very new act at the time, and he would've been newish too, although probably quite a bit more experienced than me, and already on his way to some degree of stardom. After all, he had won the BBC New Comedy Award recently and had his own solo show at the Pleasance that year too, again if my old memory serves me correctly. I believe I saw the show actually. In the Pleasance Attic, I seem to recall. Talented hardworking bastard, that he is.

Working hard is cheating is what that is. Plain and simple.

Now, at this point I think I had done a few spots at The Stand comedy clubs in Scotland, or maybe not, but I still felt fully justified in making my way along to the end of Fringe party at the Edinburgh venue on York Place. It's a bit of a Fringe institution that party, even though I haven't been in recent years. Too busy doing my own shit now, innit.

The Stand people don't mind a bit of a lash-up, so when the party at the venue died down, it was open invite time to the flat of Jane Mackay and Tommy Sheppard. They were co-founders of the The Stand, although Tommy seems to be following a more political career in bonny Scotland nowadays; a Scottish National Party politician, spokesperson to the Cabinet Office and Member of Parliament for Edinburgh East since 2015, to say the least. Jane was his partner at the time, and regular MC at the club.

The English and skinny pretty women were usually favourite subjects of Jane's to banter with (aka pick on) from the stage. All light-hearted stuff (I think), but if you are in one of those two categories, you are definitely going to get it from her! A very funny lady she was, it has to be said, but sadly I believe she went into comedy retirement a few years back. Something to do with the smoking ban in pubs and clubs.

So anyway, the taxis are all booked and it's not long before we are on our way back to Tommy and Jane's apartment.

The taxi for the people I happened to be grouped with - who I didn't really know very well at all - seemed to be one of the first responders, so I got in and back to the flat ahead of most of the others. Those others consisted of a couple of comedy mates, some comedy acquaintances and other random people I hadn't had the pleasure of meeting yet.

Upon entering the flat, and more specifically the rather nice and large kitchen area, a pleasant lady who was in my taxi saw to it that I had a bottle of beer from the fridge. Very hospitable indeed. Thank you nice lady from my taxi. One assumed she was a friend of a friend of Jane and Tommy's. I know assumptions are the mother of all fuck-ups, but I think it's a pretty safe one. And what the hell, it's a late night party. Caring is sharing, and it was beer!

Anyway, casting my mind back to all those years ago, I recall the fact that I had to filch a bottle opener from somewhere. One of those situations where everybody was looking to use it and I, somehow, had managed to procure the only device. Some vague recollection like that anyway.

So, as the other people from all the other taxis started to arrive, I'm stood in the kitchen with a beer that technically wasn't mine and a bottle opener in my hand that's being treated like gold dust.

And that's when the attack happened!

Like a seal suddenly being hit by a great white shark, I found myself the victim of a tongue lashing from an extremely irate, disgruntled and dare I say it, angry Alan Carr!

"You're so rude!!!!" I think was his opening line. Or words to that effect.
No "Hello" or anything like that.

Like the aforementioned seal would be, I was stunned!

"How dare you?!" Looking back, it was like meeting Greta Thunberg before she was born.

I had crossed paths with this chap precious few times and had always found him to be a most pleasant and agreeable fellow indeed. A totally lovely gent. It was so unexpected and confusing that I had no words. I was just trying to think what it was I could've possibly done.

And then it occurred to me, it must be the beer! After all, I hadn't brought any beers with me and had arrived at the flat even before the owners, Tommy and Jane. Alan must be thinking I have been extremely cheeky stealing somebody's beer.

And the bottle opener! Maybe it's that too? Or instead of? All these people looking for the bottle opener, and here I am having nicked it!

But surely, in my head at least, it's more likely to be the beer. But the tirade continues.

"You should be ashamed of yourself! Shame on you!"

Now Alan is no Peter Dinklage, but he's a good few inches shorter than me, and I honestly felt quite intimidated. Not just because of the confusing verbal attack, but I didn't know that many people at the party. And here I was, a marked beer thief. El Ladron de Cerveza, as they would label me in Spain.

Still, I suppose with retrospect it would've been quite funny to any onlookers, having this shortish bespectacled camp bloke shouting up at a mixed race bloke in a baseball cap. Not that anyone saw it. I don't think.

Still, I hung around for a bit and then about half an hour later, I saw Alan approaching again.

Was I in for a second helping of verbal abuse? Yet another

'Carr Clash'? Albeit that last one being rather one-sided. I didn't know what to think or say.

Then he surprised me again, as he arrived at where I was standing. "I'm terribly sorry," he exclaimed.

Again, I had no words. What was he apologising for? I mean, I still had the guilty gold dust bottle opener in my hand. Perhaps another one had been found?

So, slightly baffled yet again, I queried as to what I was told off and then forgiven for? I'd been made to feel guilty and then forgiven and know not what I've done. I'm not even catholic!

Then he went on to say, "I heard somebody was slagging me off in one of the taxis back here and I thought it was you!"

"Oh....right. Nope, definitely not me," I replied.

"I know, so I apologise. Please forgive me."

"Sure, no worries"

"They were saying I shouldn't have won the BBC New Comedy Award. That I didn't deserve it. What's wrong with people?"

I agreed with him that there was no need for such bitterness and his apology was happily accepted. I mean, Alan is very good comedian and lovely bloke after all.

To this day, I am still baffled as to how I could've been confused with somebody else since I was the only tall mixed-race person at the party, but there you go.

Now, cut forward a couple of years into the future, and I had a gig in the Manchester area and drove up with Shelley Cooper. Shelley is a transgender comedian and one of the nicest people I've met on the comedy circuit, so I thoroughly enjoyed her company and her stories of being in the army and her trials for

Chelsea FC before having the operation. Tales of her background were fascinating.

I picked her up at her place and we set off after a cup of cha. She asked if it was ok if we stop off at somebody's house on the way to the gig. She needed to pick something up from there that she had left when she'd stayed over recently… apparently.

It was the home of none other than Mr Alan Carr! The one and the same, who had not only blasted and forgiven me some time ago, but was well on his way to a prosperous TV career.

Shelley knocked and Alan opened the door. As soon as he saw Shelley there were the customary hellos and hugs before he set eyes on me. "You know Nik, don't you?" Shelley said.

I never like to assume anybody remembers me from a few brief encounters years back, but then Alan surprised me again.

"I do…" he replied to Shelley, "And I must apologise!" he said and put one hand over his mouth and the other over his heart. Again, slight confusion for me. "What now?' I thought! "I can't believe I had a go at you at that Stand after party!" he went on, "For something you didn't even do! I'm so so sorry! I hope you forgive me."

I smiled and said, "No worries dude," as we shook hands and proceeded into his house to pick up Shelley's umbrella.

That was over TWO YEARS previously! And he remembered! And apologised again.

I like that Alan Carr bloke, even if he's never likely to have me on his chat show.

Long before Greta...

Chapter 5 - Comedians Thrash Hibernian FC!

Future stars can also be seen playing games of football, as well as on stage and at festival closing parties.

Now, I believe it was during the Edinburgh Fringes of 2008 and 2009 that some crazy bastard decided to arrange a Sunday morning game of football at stupid o'clock against Hibernian FC. That fool being me.

It was for charity, of course. The big deal being that every comedian who took part in the game, if they were doing a Free Festival show, donates the proceeds from the voluntary donations of their solo show bucket collection to the charity.

I would like to remember which charity it was, but I can barely remember what year. I have a vague recollection of it being an organisations that helps homeless people that have gotten into drugs and the like back into a more normal life and the workplace.

The funny thing was that one comedian in particular always used to brag about how massive his bucket collection was at his solo show, but miraculously had his lowest ever takings that night. What possibly could've happened? Who can say for sure, but we could all smell something in the air. Not that we couldn't with regards to his boasting most days anyway.

That's the thing about pathological liars. People know they are full of it. We can all smell the bullshit. It's just ironic that they tell porkies to make people think they are cool, but the very thing they are doing to make people think that they are cool is the very thing that ultimately makes them look totally the opposite and more like a dick.

Anyway, said game was to take place on a Sunday morning about halfway through the Festival. Yep, we all had to meet at 9:30am outside Edinburgh City Football Club just down from the Playhouse Theatre. At the time it was a Free Festival venue, but I believe that venue is no more. The football club, not the Playhouse Theatre. The theatre is very much alive and well.

We met there because it was on Leith Walk, which was in the direction of the where we were due to play.

I say 'we met there' and we eventually did but only after Yours Truly spent 20 minutes on the phone at 9:30am on a Sunday morning trying to find out where the hungover comedians were!

I do have to report that the first game in 2008 ended with Hibs winning 6-5. Which when you think about it, considering we were playing a Scottish Premier League football team, isn't too bad for a bunch of fuzzy-headed hungover comedians after a Saturday night at the Edinburgh Fringe.

Especially given we only had nine men! Actually, I tell a lie, one was a woman; Gill Smith. Because let's face it, we do not discriminate! And to be even more honest, she was actually one of the better players! Probably by virtue of the fact that she was fitter than most of us and not a pisshead.

You must be thinking, how would nine cobbled together drunk comedians put five goals past the mighty Hibernian FC? Well, I guess we are better players than you would think.

Ok, ok, so I confess! It was the Hibernian FC under-17 girls team!

Now you may laugh, but let me tell you, those girls were shit hot on the ball. Sparkling professional-looking green kits, organised and not one of them took any shit! I want to call them 'young ladies' but I can't. At times, they were bloody brutal. Calculating, dirty, fouling, brutal young women. With toughness levels the like of which you'd see shouting, screaming and head-butting their way along Sauchiehall Street on a night out in Glasgow! Only fitter.

This all came about because myself and some of the other acts were all good friends with the lovely and hilarious comedian JoJo Sutherland. I say 'lovely', but 'tis best not to get on her bad side, or you'll soon find yourself on the business end of some verbal abuse. Not that I have felt such wrath (much) myself, but trust me when I tell you never to let JoJo know any secrets, because if she knows, everybody knows. I've certainly found that out the hard way. 'Foggy' I like to call her, on account of the fact she has a mouth like a Foghorn. If she was a cartoon character, it would certainly be the giant rooster, Foghorn Leghorn.

JoJo's daughter Ciara played for the team. Like most of the players, but probably the worst of all, Ciara took it all very seriously. Competitive, deadly and wanting to win at all costs.

And of course, they did!

We did actually have eleven players on the pitch in the end, because Hibernian turned up with the full eleven players plus subs, so given we were all a bit fucked, we roped in a couple of 10-year-old Scottish lads who happened to be there in the park.

Our team talk with the boys was simple…
"Listen kids. We are old, drunk and slow. So, your job is to chase the girls all around the pitch and when you get the ball off them, pass it to one of us."

And they did! They ran their arses off for the full 90 minutes as we huffed and puffed through the game and somehow managed to get five goals. We could've got a few more actually, if the then not-yet-famous Scottish comedian Daniel Sloss could actually get a shot on target!

He was in his late teens at the time, so probably the fittest amongst us, so a quick ball over the top for him to run onto was another game plan. But every time he was through, the twat put the ball 10 metres over the crossbar! Could not hit the proverbial cow's arse with a banjo. Still, he was a very enthusiastic young man. So much so, that at one point during the match - and I'm quite sure he won't thank me for telling you this - he went up for a one-on-one with one of the girls, and accidentally head-butted her in the face. Well, I say 'accidentally'. Only he knows the truth of what his true intentions were. Maybe it was some teenage mating ritual that we were not privy to.

Of course, our loss was not helped by a couple of dubious incidents. If memory serves me correctly, at one point we were actually ahead 2 - 1, but our goalkeeper at the time, one Craig Shaynak, for some inexplicable reason, raised his foot up from a simple, slow back-pass and the ball went straight underneath it and into the back of the net. The true irony being that given the accuracy of the back-pass, if he would've just stood there and done nothing, the ball would've actually stopped at his foot, ready for him to kick out into the field again.

Craig, who I'm sure won't mind me telling you this, is a rather large American comedy actor who usually favours not moving at all. So why he decided to make any kind of move-ment on this occasion was beyond all of us. Maybe he had received the so-called 'brown envelope' before the game started?

FYI, as well as a couple of great solo shows at Fringes both in Edinburgh and Hollywood, Craig has had starring roles - albeit smaller ones - in a number of Hollywood productions, most notably the TV show Ray Donovan and movie Ted 2. I love the Ted movies by the way. Hilarious tear-inducing comedies, they are for me. In the latter, Ted 2, he was the fat blind guy at the bar who got a biscuit thrown in-between his arse cheeks. Not a big role, but a memorable one. Big arse too. And memorable.

I love the word 'biscuit' too. I don't know why, but it amuses me every time I hear the word. Hence I've used that, rather than the American 'cookie'.

The second dubious moment, being a penalty kick incident with the game finely balanced at 5 - 5, going into the last few minutes. Donald Mack, who was playing centre-back decided to plough right through a 15-year-old girl advancing towards our goal, after she out-paced the panting smoker.

Chopper Harris would've been proud of that tackle.

So obviously, the referee blew up for a penalty kick. Donald threw his arms up in disgust at the ref's decision, claiming that he got the ball. But without VAR at the time, a big scary black man scything down a young Scottish girl was always going to go in Hibernian's favour. I do use the term 'big scary black man' to describe Donald Mack, but to be honest, that couldn't be further from the truth.

Donald will try to pretend he is a super cool black guy, but he is quite soppy and cuddly really. But compared to their small centre forward, he did look a bit large and frightening. I mean, she and the referee wouldn't know what a playful soppy wanker he is in his everyday life, would they?

Still, the penalty kick was given and it was of course converted. I dare say she'd practised a few penalty kicks on the training ground, after all. And that was that.

We went down 6 - 5 to a bunch of schoolgirls. Given their level of regular football training and general fitness, I don't think we need to be too ashamed. Especially when the referee confessed back in the clubhouse to seeing that Donald actually won the ball!

Another bastard who probably got a brown envelope before the game started!

However, it was all jolly good fun and we did agree with the referee that you shouldn't really be putting in such a tackle on a female player half your size. Yes, screw you Donald, that was a harsh move and you cost us the game. Bastard. Well, you and the biscuit-bummed Hollywood 'star' in goal.

However, one year on and we decided to have a rematch. We also decided to have a little bit of a training session on the Meadows a couple of days before the game, not get pissed the night before and on the day and have a full strength team with substitutes!

Learning from our mistakes! Go us!

It was also arranged for us to play at Meadowbank Stadium, so a massive upgrade from the park in Craigiehall!

The nice people at Hibernian had a proper kit for us and everything!

And not to blow my own trumpet, but I ran that centre midfield like a God, spraying the ball around all over the place and we ran out 5 - 0 winners. Zico, Pirlo, Zidane, Maradona, Platini, all eat your hearts out! Coppin was on fire! I don't mind telling you that I scored a couple of crackers as well.

At 2 - 0, JoJo's vicious daughter Ciara was going crazy, with a face that looked like hell at its most furious, she was absolutely fuming. And the more pissed off she got, the more we enjoyed the game. Elbowing and kicking ankles throughout the game she was.

Ciara took the defeat well.

But Ciara wasn't the only one that was being overly-competitive. At one point, one of the 15-year-old players put herself in an ambulance! By that, I don't mean she just walked into it. That would be silly. She actually went in so hard on a tackle with Paul

Nik 'Pele' Coppin with my captain's big silver trophy.
Take that, Ciara!

Ricketts, that she done herself such an injury an ambulance needed to be called and take her to the local infirmary.

It was totally of her own doing, but of course we've never let Paul Ricketts forget the fact that he put a teenage girl in hospital. Bastard. Especially since he was the only player that was from the Free Fringe, whereas most of us were Free Festival, with a couple of acts from other venues.

Getting me going about the 'Free Festival' v the 'Free Fringe' is certainly not something to do right now. The differences and rivalry over the years is a book all of its own.

In the end, the girls' competitiveness was in vain of course, because our much more organised outfit took the game five goals to zero. After that, they didn't seem to want to play the following year. But they did give us a nice big silver trophy, which was used later in a solo show, Award-Winning Comedian, Nik Coppin. A show about all the non-comedy awards I'd won. And to add to our smugness and overall joy, JoJo reported back to us that for the rest of the night, her daughter was slamming doors and smashing the place up.

Despite the fact we remain friends, I think that Ciara still holds her crushing defeat against me. In fact, I am sure she does.

But what the hell, we get to say that a bunch of comedians thrashed the mighty Hibernian FC, five goals to nil. And of course, we rarely add the caveat that it was a team under of 17-year-old girls.

"The fact we only won 6-5 the first game pissed me off, so to actually lose 5-0 the following year I was ready to kick Nik square in the nuts. I can genuinely say I was like the Monk out of Mean Machine taking bodies left, right and centre. And 10 years later I can genuinely say I'm over it… kind of. Nik however is holding on to his only moment of glory… he is after all an Arsenal fan so he needs to hold on to some footballing happiness. Prick!"

Ciara Donaldson

Chapter 6 - The Price Is Wrong

I've said it once and I'll say it again. Comedians can't be trusted and can be right bastards.

A few years ago at the Edinburgh Fringe, I was MCing every day at one of the Laughing Horse Pick of the Fringe line-up shows and one Matthew Eric Price was doing regular spots at the show.

On more than one occasion, sorry, let me correct myself, loads of occasions, Matt Price would get the audience to join him in heckling me that Wolverine would beat Spider-Man in a fight.

I would often have to come on stage and deal with an on-slaught of geek and non-geek audience members alike telling me that Spider-Man would meet defeat in such a tussle.

Of course, they are wrong. And the more sensible members of the crowd would be on my side. Spider-Man for the victory.

Of course, a lot of female members of the audience would go for Wolverine. They like Wolverine, you see. Well, I say 'Wolver-ine', but let's face it, they just fancy Hugh Jackman. And certain-ly in more recent years, in their minds they would be pitting Hugh Jackman against Tom Holland. Not taking into account the powers involved with both characters.

However, I reckon Tom Holland would give him a right old doing anyway. British versus Australian, innit? Brit's got to win.

That, and I've done shows with Spider-Man's dad. That's right, British comedian and author Dominic Holland, being the father of young Tom. The last time I met Mr Dominic, we both

did Edinburgh previews together in Piccadilly. Rather amusingly, at least 60% of the audience were young women in their 20s
dressed in things like skintight Black Widow and other eye-
catching superhero-based attire. Clearly geeky fans of Spider-
Man, Marvel and of course fancying Tom clearly hoping to catch
the attention of daddy Dom.

Like, what do they think is going to happen? They laugh at
Tom's dad, and he arranges for them to be his daughter-in-law?
It's all very sweet, but a little bit strange when a middle-aged
man talking about middle-aged married man issues is playing to
young 20-year-old female geeks.

So, that fucker Matt Price took great pleasure throughout the
entire month of August in rallying the Wolverine troops to shout
at me that the hairy little runt could take down the amazing
Wallcrawler.

And yes, Wolverine is just that. A hairy little runt of a man.
Sure, Hugh Jackman has been a great servant to the superhero
cause and a fantastic 'Hollywood Wolverine', but in real life - the
comic books - Logan is 5'3" tall, stocky, extremely hairy, smokes
cigars and drinks grog all the time. Not like the 5'10" tall, athletic, hazel-eyed lovely man that is Peter Parker.

So let's put this into perspective for you all and set things
straight for the record. First of all, Wolverine is a fast healer, this
power creep regeneration nonsense got ridiculous. Wolverine
can die. There are some people that would have you believe
if the planet Earth blew up, Wolverine would be floating around
in space for all eternity. Probably with Keith Richards. Storylines

where Wolverine has regenerated from just a few cells, or put himself back together after being ripped in half by the Incredible Hulk are just, well, foolishness and rubbish lazy writing.

With massive blood loss, severe burning and lack of oxygen, the X-Man can and will meet his end. In fact, I found out an interesting fact recently. If you did cut off Wolverine's air supply, like in a drowning situation, due to his healing factor, the whole process would take a considerable amount longer than a regular person and therefore prove to be an extremely lengthy and hor-ribly painful process for him. I'm not the torturous kind, but I couldn't help find that quite interesting and amusing.

Blimey, maybe I really am a bit of a sadistic wanker.

But sure, I agree, Wolverine would in fact be very hard to kill, and is a lot more used to killing people than the law-abiding Spider-Man, who would prefer to arrest rather than bump off. We do need to remember of course that Wolverine is actually a hero too and doesn't kill people unnecessarily. But in a fight to the death, I still think Spider-Man, if he absolutely had to kill, would still be triumphant.

Of course, if Spider-Man had to stand toe-to-toe with Wolvie, the runt's chances of victory would go up significantly. But Spider-Man is still way faster and way stronger than Wolverine. Wolvie actually has no superhuman strength or speed. Stronger and faster than your regular human being of course, but Spidey is fast enough to dodge bullets, so how hard would it be for him to evade what are essentially six steak knives that can't even be thrown at him?

I mean, they are pretty amazing steak knives, it has to be said. An adamantium set would last a lifetime of cutting up rib-eyes and sirloins. Wouldn't say no to those in me kitchen.

The Webhead can also lift somewhere in the region of 10 tons. So I'm sure that a man who can benchpress a double-decker bus wouldn't have too much trouble tearing our short hirsute friend limb from limb. Lest we forget that Wolvie's joints aren't laced with adamantium after all. Of course, Spider-Man would find that sort of action incredibly unsavoury and would rather choose not do it. But the point being, he just could.

He would probably rather utilise his long-range weapons, yep, his web shooters. With those nifty bits of technology he could easily immobilise Wolverine from a distance, rendering all movement impossible and therefore use of his claws redundant. He could quite simply tie him up and give him a good spanking. Literally.

Oh, and there is also the little matter of his Spider Sense, warning him of any and all impending danger. So, Spider-Man for the win. A vote for Wolverine in such a contest, would be like a vote for the Lib Dems in a UK General Election. Completely and utterly wasted and foolish.

You know, don't think I suffer from some Spidey bias and believe he would beat everybody in a fight. Like, Batman, yep, Captain America, sure, Daredevil, easy, but the likes of the The Hulk and Superman? No, no, no, no, no. Definitely not. The latter is both way faster and way stronger than Spidey and whilst his superior speed would give him some advantages over the not-so-jolly green giant, the Hulk's endurance, near indestructibility and limitless strength would simply prove too much.

But then you are always going to get somebody that throws a completely ridiculous one into the mix. A good Adelaidean budkin of mine Pete 'The Titch' Titchener, did such a thing at my solo show during the Fringe there. I met Titch the first year I did the Fringe in 2009. He reviewed my show that year and because he said good things, I allowed him to be a mate.

I'm nice like that.

But the following year, he returned and started heckling me that Spider-Man would lose in a fight to his unusual personal hero, the Great Train Robber - Ronnie Biggs!

What absolute poppycock!

Only a madman would say such a thing. Or someone with some serious insecurities. I mean to have an infamous British criminal as your hero is weird enough, but it's probably why he's called 'Titch'. Tiny penis, innit? Admittedly that's a nickname I use for him myself and to my knowledge, nobody else uses it, but a man with a tiny cock is a man with a tiny cock.

And he's a folk musician too, so what would he know? He's a good folk musician, I'll grant him that. But what would a man who sings and strums the 'music of the people' know about such important matters like which superhero would beat which superhero? Still, 'Titchy Willy' amused me enough with his foolish match-up heckling that I knocked up a drawing for him that hangs in his tool garage to this day.

"Little dick Wolverine couldn't even catch gonorrhoea!"

And it hangs a lot better than some other things about his person, of that much I'm certain.

Rant over.

Actually, no, it's not. Turns out at some point towards the end of the Edinburgh Fringe, Matt Price confessed to me that it was actually another comedian matey, Gareth Berliner, who following a recent car journey discussion about such matters, was going around sneakily telling people that if they bump into me they should all wind me about the fact that Wolverine would beat Spider-Man.

Like I said, comedians, bastards.

As it happens, Mr Matt Price does a rather popular podcast called 'Conversations With Criminals'. Basically, he's been all over the UK, Europe and the world interviewing people that have, shall we say, a shady past. It is very interesting and insightful, I have to say. Not that he ever mentions it, but you should check it out.

And actually, if the grey matter remembers rightly, Matt even went to Ronnie Biggs funeral!

That being said, since one of Spidey and Wolvie's most famous comic book ding-dongs took place in a graveyard in Berlin, maybe Marvel comics should do a follow-up which sees old Ronnie rising from 6-foot under to have tussle with them?

A right old Royal Rumble that would be.

Spider-Man would win, of course.

Silly ideas aside and with a bit of retrospect, maybe it's people that have a love and affinity to the criminal underworld that tend to go against Spider-Man.

Whereas the people that tend to go for the Webslinger are good, honest, law-abiding citizens like myself.

That must be it.

Chapter 7 - Spider-Man: The Greatest Superhero of Them All... PROVED!

Alright everybody, calm down! Courtesy of the dream I just had during an afternoon snooze, I think I have the answer to that age-old debate...

Who is the greatest superhero of all time?

So there is this young mutant woman who is immensely powerful. Like, Omega-level celestial powers. But she is afraid to use them, and is frightened and nervous.

Other than the destruction she can cause with her abilities, she is also scared because she has an angry determined Wolverine tracking her down to kill her. Luckily, she happens to bump into everybody's friendly neighbourhood amazing Spider-Man (the greatest superhero ever btw)... In the English countryside of all places, just on the outskirts of London.

After several double-decker bus journeys and on more than one occasion Spider-Man punching and kicking an advancing Wolverine through a few bus windows, some good hard talking and explaining calms the situation down and everybody gets on in the end.

And there you have it. There is nothing that can't be sorted out with a good bit of negotiation and open-mindedness.

They all sit down on a nice park bench and table combo in close quarters, to have a picnic together. But not before Wolverine bows down to the greatness of Spider-Man, who has webbed up his claws to sit directly opposite because in Spidey's words, "You're still a bit of a mad fucker after all!"

Well, they were my words actually because I was in the suit. I don't like to use such words, but what better way to describe Wolverine.

You won't get that from any other mixed race Spider-Man, Mr Miles Morales.

Chapter 8 - The Worst Gig Ever?

Only thing worse than bastard comedians, is a bastard audience. Even though the bad gigs make good stories. Comedy is tragedy plus time after all.

Because let's face it, there is no joy to be had in telling a load of stories where the gig went great and you ripped it apart and brought the house down. There are always those comedians that can't wait to tell you how well they have done. Most of the time, they bore you senseless with their self aggrandising with regard to how great they have been.

"They loved me!", "I killed!", "I roofed it!". Yada, yada, yada. Yawn, yawn, yawn.

It's all rubbish really, but fortunately for the sanity of us all, they are in the minority.

The best times and conversations with fellow comedians are when you and your comedy comrades talk about the times you went down like the Hindenburg in a room with some of the most horrendous audiences imaginable.

Most circuit comedians have at least one or two stories of such happenings at a Jongleurs show. Jongleurs being a chain of comedy clubs that marketed its shows largely to stag and hen parties, which I believe at the height of its powers had about 17 regular clubs all over the UK from as far south as the shit fight of the Portsmouth gig, up through varying degrees of niceness and toughness in London, the Midlands - Nottingham probably being the most horrible there, the north-west and a couple of rather tricky ones in Glasgow and Edinburgh. Not that I ever played any gigs at those latter two.

Shame, because I do love a gig in Bonny Scotland.

But of course, Jongleurs is no more. After flapping and floundering around like a fish on the deck of a fishing vessel struggling to breathe for far too long, trying to save itself from financial ruin whilst ripping a load of comedians off as it was doing so (editor's note - allegedly), it finally died a death. The stories of how this chain treated comedians and how comedians allowed themselves to be treated is perhaps for another time. And I must remember to tell you about the maggots sometime!

That being said with regard to the financial skulduggery, there were plenty of fantastic nights had over weekends with

Jongleurs and many hilarious tales of good comedians crashing and burning before the drunken stag and hen parties. And the Christmas shows. Oh what a joy... Not! Always nice to receive the cheque at the end of those weeks, which helped to numb the pain of your dignity being crushed in front of 300 people that really couldn't give a shit about some twat talking on stage.

The Hyena club in Newcastle was another one of those notoriously tough clubs. It could be hell on toast dealing with all the birthday parties and stags and hens. And just like Jongleurs, sadly that club is no more, which really is a shame, because as rough as it could be, it was a right old laugh and Yvonne, who used to book the comedians, was one of the loveliest women you could ever meet. Always marvellous to deal with, very friendly and up for a few laughs and beverages after the show.

She was also the sister of Dave Johns who I believe started the club many moons ago. Davey Johns being of recent movie fame having played the lead role in 'I, Daniel Blake', which won the Palme d'Or at the Cannes Film Festival in 2016 for best movie. Not that he ever mentions any of that, of course.

So, speaking of destinations in the more southerly locations of European countries, Torremolinos.

A little while back, a very good friend and comedy promoter by the name of Paul Redwood decided he was going to buy a bar in the Torremolinos area of Spain.

I knew Paul from doing the comedy gigs he ran on our lovely south coast and gigged for him on a number of occasions, often crashing out in a flat that he lived in above a bingo hall in

Shirley (that's a place, not a woman) where he was manager. A few beers after the gig, back to the bingo flat to get one's head down, then a delicious free breakfast in the morning whilst watching the blue rinse brigade get angry because Ethel won that particular round on her bingo card.

Don't fuck with granny, man!

After a couple of visits to Spain and Paul shifting from one bar to another, we decided to put on a little comedy show at his venue. I said I would do it if he came out of retirement and did the show with me. He did and he was surprisingly pretty good given he hadn't gigged for ages. It was a lovely little show with 15 people in the audience, including Jo and Mark who co-owned the 'Event and Grill' bar with him and who were a most lovely couple indeed, a few other people and my good friend who I often stay with in Berlin, Doreen.

My giant-headed friend Tony who I have known for years sadly missed the show because he didn't arrive until the next day. Poor Tony.

However, the next time I visited in the May of 2018, Paul thought it might be a good idea for me to do another comedy set. This time not at his bar, but at the bar of a woman who had recently purchased a place not far from his. Amanda was her name, and like many bar owners in that part of the world, she was struggling to get people in and make a few euros, so she thought it might be good to have a comedy show on her birthday.

A birthday comedy show in a bar to a load of expats in Torremolinos? The thought of playing table tennis with my own testicles would be more appealing. It however came to light that for reasons I won't bore you with, she'd brought in another comedian and promoter by the name of Geoff Whiting to do the show. So given that I was there to see me mate Paul as well as hanging out with three other old mateys whom I knew from my 'working' on the London Underground days, I tried to wriggle my way out of what would undoubtedly be a soul-destroying experience. The three mates from my previous working life being Tony Hadlames, the bloke with the massive noggin who had missed my last gig in Spain, Kebba Jobe and Freddy Morris. But more about those twats later.

I mean really, why would I put myself through the absolute Purgatory of playing to a bunch of British and Irish drunken birthday partying expats when you've got Geoff to do it anyway? I could just come and watch the horrendously amusing situation unfold, with a beer in one hand and a packet of crisps in the other, thanking the comedy gods that it's not me up there.

But for some ridiculous reason against my better judgement, I agreed to do the gig after a phone call between myself and Amanda whilst I was still in Melbourne doing the comedy festival there. Still, being the all-round good egg (head) that I am and Amanda seeming quite lovely, if it helps her financially to keep her bar going, why not? A fool and his dignity are soon parted.

After all, as the old saying goes, no good deed goes unpunished. And that was certainly the case with this 'favour'.

First of all, the set up was completely wrong. The show was to be in a long bar with those sofas connected to the wall all along one side, with a load of tables with chairs in and outside the bar, of which most of the chairs weren't even facing the stage which was to be on a chessboard-style dance floor in front of the bar.

Of course, you can't really blame Amanda because how is she to know how a comedy show should be set up. But Geoff's then partner, Anita, who also ran an agency said she would sort the seating to make it a more playable show. I think she must have moved one or two chairs to point them in the direction of the stage and that was it. Thanks Anita!

Paul, who again had to agree to MC the show, went up and did quite a grand job of attempting to get people listening. Then Geoff, who must be some kind of masochist, decided to do about 40 minutes in front of the largely indifferent audience which consisted of about 50 or 60 people. Throwing in a large amount of re-worked old jokes from the 1970's, he managed a few chuckles.

To paint a clear picture of how dreadful the audience were, the only person - or thing rather - that actually paid any real attention to the show and looked to be enjoying itself, was an Alsatian sat on one of the sofa things. So yes, not just any dog, but a German dog! Of course, I would rather refer to it as a 'thing', because it was the least animal-like being in the audience.

At this stage in proceedings I'm hoping against hope that those jokes only got titters because they would be up for something a little more contemporary. Yep, the hopes and expectations of a madman. Like a condemned criminal waiting to be led to the gallows hoping against hope that the rope snaps. But there's always another rope.

A 45-minute interval followed Geoff, and during that time said patrons threw more and more alcohol down their Gregory Peck's, which was never going to bode well for the second half. My imminent death became more likely when half the audience decided to leave and were replaced by a 30-strong crowd who had been at the wake of one of Amanda's friend's dad's funeral a couple of bars down the road. In the words of Shere Khan the tiger from the Disney classic movie, The Jungle Book, "How delightful." And at this stage I think I'd rather have him in the audience... claws and all.

Now, I mention Mr Khan because as those that know me are aware, he is a staple of one of my routines. A routine that largely fell on uncaring indifferent ears on this night. Right up until the punchline, which did get a laugh albeit rather dishearteningly. But we will get to that.

So after my mate Paul did his best to get the audience under control, my death march towards the stage began. Of course, to assist Paul, and to avert my certain upcoming death, I did my best to try to stop people talking at the bar as well. Those people being three rather large blokes, the biggest of which had what can only be described as a scary Northern Irish accent, as he looked down at me and rather aggressively said, "So we're not even allowed to order drinks at the bar now?!"

Oooooo-kay, so I'm going to leave this situation alone, I thought to myself. The last thing I need to compound what is already going to be a nightmare, is three large blokes raining down heckles from across the room. But no sooner have I taken to the chessboard stage, than the three large individuals decide to come and plant themselves in the three empty seats directly in front of me. The hits, as they say, just keep on coming!

I start with an upbeat and friendly, but slightly nervous, "Hello Torremolinos" to which I get a quite muted response. But whatever, I'll hit them with a few of me best bankers and then ride the wave of those for the next 20 to 30 minutes.

So, out comes the 'MASSIVE BLACK ONE! That would be one of my more regular jokes by the way, not showing the audience my penis. That wouldn't be massive. Or black. Well, not completely black anyway.

A couple of titters throughout the room at most! What?! I mean, it's not the best joke in the world, but it rarely falls that flat! So, feeling like a boxer who has just caught someone with his best right hook flush on the chin with little to no effect I'm really on the back foot, so I bring another few big boys out. Mostly about what little sex stuff I have and Germans, with their lack of a sense of humour. The Brits and Irish will like that. Wrong! Not even titters this time!

This is not good. With at least another 20 minutes that I should be doing in front of some rather judgemental expat eyes, along with the the knowledge that my three twatty friends are looking on from the back, I must do something. Especially since they are the sort of 'friends' that even if you rip a gig apart, they will tell you that you were shit.

So as any comedian worth their salt will tell you, connecting with the audience in front of you is paramount to having a good gig. Especially if you can get the biggest bloke in the room on your side. As such, I turn my attention to the man from the bar to establish some good old-fashioned banter.

"So, you're from Northern Ireland?" "No."

Thinking he must be having me on and might actually be up for a bit of playful banter, I go on. "Come on man, I know a Northern Irish accent when I hear one."

"I'm not from Northern Ireland!", he reiterates, wanting to make it perfectly clear that he is not up for any kind of jovial banter whatsoever.

So I think to myself, "Fuck him," and turn my attention to a large table of people just behind him and his mates. Now I know from the first half where this table are from, so to have a nice little dig at the ignorant bastard sat in front of me I open the conversation with, "So, you are from the real Ireland?"

They nod, and the death stare that I get from the big bloke sat right in front of me suggests he was in fact lying about his country of origin all along. Too late, Mr Northern Ireland, you had your chance. And admittedly, I could've had my potato chips if he would've kicked off. But fuck him. And he didn't, so there.

I go on chatting to the Republic of Ireland crew and focus my attention on the matriarch of the table who seems to be in charge of the group and ask her what she does for a living. She responds! "I work in forensics."

Ooh, interesting… so I says "Like the TV show then, CSI?"

"I suppose so, yes," she replies again in her dulcet Irish lilt.

So, given the demographic of the room, i.e. with the exception of the odd Scandinavian and Spaniard, English, Scottish Welsh and Irish, I feel an opportunity to whip up a nice bit of friendly home countries rivalry.

"Yeah, so like, instead of CSI in America, it would be CSI: Ireland. Only difference being, every single episode, the English did it!" Nothing! Not even a titter!

Come! On! Admittedly it's not my best ever witty retort, but given the history and banter between the two nations and what I'm up against, I thought that was quite quick and reasonably clever. It certainly deserved something!

But no. Fuck all!

Not even from the seemingly friendly Scouse bloke that I've had banter with before the show started. I'm quite certain that the Irish table, not picking up on my subtle reference, thought I was having a real go at them. Equally, my fellow English people in the room no doubt thought I was having a right go at them, so now the death stares are raining down from Northern Ireland, the Republic of Ireland and my home country of England!

Marvellous.

So, with a rising sense of desperation, panic and fear, even though it's all rather amusing, no doubt especially to my wanky mates sat just outside, I throw out a lifeline to a middle-aged Scottish woman.

I mean, as I said previously, I always tend to have a good time north of the border at the Edinburgh Fringe and pretty much every other gig I've done in bonny Scotland. So surely the Scottish lady will help me turn the gig around.

"What part of Scotland are you from?" I enquire in my best Scottish accent. Which is pretty good if I do say so myself.

"Glasgow," she answers.

Now I know from experience that the Glaswegians love a bit of banter and are more than willing to laugh about the rough and ready reputation of said city, so I follow up with, "Blimey, bit rough in Glasgow, isn't it?"which will lead nicely into my bit about that big cartoon stripey cat I mentioned earlier.

With a rather aggressive Glasgow accent, or as I like to call it, a Glasgow accent, she replies, "No! It's not!"

So, no Scottish rescue for me then. Hence, I decide to double down because fuck it, I'm here now and I've got my routine ready to go. A routine that does work time and time again I should add. Because who doesn't love impressions of what Disney characters should sound like?

"Yes it is! I've been there!" I say, almost as though she knows nothing of her home city. She's probably spent too much time having her Celtic brain cells frazzled by the Spanish sun.

Scottish stares. Irish stares. English stares. There may have been some Welsh stares, but I didn't establish if any of our cousins from the valleys were in.

Given such eyeballing, I have to make what I would consider to be no more than a passing comment "This is going great, isn't?" Laughs! From pretty much everybody. Schadenfreude! Bunch of expat bastards! Laughing at my comedic misfortune! But laughter nonetheless and at least it relieves some of the rising tension in the room.

With that, I begin my routine which those who have seen it starts with the referencing of Glasgow people being a bit tapped, especially after a few sherbets, and you shouldn't mess with them, then proceeds on to observe the fact that many villains in movies and more especially Disney movies, have English accents. Like I said, everybody likes an impression or two, don't they?

The Disney bit starts with Scar from the Lion King, passes through Jafar from Aladdin and the evil priest in The Hunchback Of Notre-Dame, takes a bit of a swerve over to Hans Gruber from Die Hard, who are all African, Middle-Eastern, French and German respectively yet have English accents, and ends on the aforementioned Shere Khan from the Jungle Book. The latter being probably the most evil of all due to wanting to hunt and kill a small boy. Sly, calculating and again, an English accent! He lives in the jungle of India!

As such after doing what I think is a rather decent rendition of the George Sanders voiceover, I give him the correct accent.

Indian. This, of all the material in front of this apathetic at best audience, draws a degree of laughter. Now, the keener comedy eye will appreciate that there is a subtle undercurrent of looking at how we subconsciously stereotype people, how they act and how they speak.

An English accent - and especially one more posh in its delivery - is observed to be more sinister, whereas an Indian accent is seen as more comical, therefore an evil tiger with such an accent would sound simply too silly to want to murder a small child. Given the choice I think maybe I'd prefer the latter stereotype, but each to their own.

But with what I think I realised with my amateur psychological eye, was this bunch of ne'er-do-wells along the Costa Del Crime were almost certainly laughing at what they likely see as a race of people beneath them. Xenophobic emigrant twats. With that, I called it a day after about 17 minutes, leaving my friend and MC Paul to wrap up the 'comedy' proceedings and took myself to the bar for what I thought would be the promised free drinks. Amanda's visiting, bar-tending daughter didn't seem to be aware of this deal however and I wasn't going to make it an issue. I just want to guzzle some amber nectar down as rapidly as possible before facing the inexpert comedy critics; Tony, Kebba and Freddy.

Two pints and out I go to face the piss-taking music.

"Did you get paid for that?!" I believe was the first question from Tony. The portly white one of the three with the ginormous napper, who makes it clear that if I got paid one penny it would be a penny too much.

It was €70 that I was offered, along with some free drinks that I never got, but as I point out, "I was never going to take the money off Amanda."

"And rightly so!" Freddy chips in.

Freddy is a tall black guy who doesn't like to disclose his age, but we know he's in his late 50's. Maybe 60 now. Old bastard. He has a gold tooth, wears fishnet vests and looks a bit like if Frank Bruno lost a few inches off his height, but put a good few into his belly. Probably got a tiny penis too. I reckon all three of them have.

Freddy, being the black Don Juan De Marco that he thinks he is, suggested that I only took the gig because I fancied Amanda. She was an attractive lady in her early 50's, but I can assure you that it was in fact Freddy trying his sleazy hand at doing the wild thing with the landlady. And failing miserably of course. Well, Freddy and the gruff old Swedish bloke who looked like Captain Jean-Luc Picard, who wanted to beat me up because he got upset about me pointing out the fact he wanted to chat up Amanda as well.

"You can't take dosh off her after that shit, especially on her birthday!" Freddy continued.

With that, Kebba returns to the table from the bar with a round of drinks in his hands. Kebba is the largest of all of us and probably cops the most flack with regard to his over-eating and love of a Wetherspoons' mixed grill when the all-too-often

Fat Freddy Morris

childish blokey banter takes place. He is a mixed race chap a year younger and a few stone heavier than me, so in effect he could be my little big (massive) brother. His mix of races - like my fellow comedian and friend Bruce Fummey - is Scottish-African, whereas mine is English-Caribbean. So I do enjoy a bit of race-based rivalry badinage with both these guys from time-to-time.

It's all very puerile indeed. But fun.

Following on from what Freddy and Tony have commented, Kebba chimes in, "No man, you have to take the money!"

I'm starting to think I might have not just an ally in my little massive brother, but also somebody that understands the fact that comedy is not an exact science and rather subjective and therefore you should take the money regardless of how good or bad you've done on any given comedy night.

Kebba goes on, "Because it's Amanda's birthday right?"

"Yep."

"Well, if you do a gig for her on her birthday for free, that's like a birthday present, isn't it?" he adds. "I suppose so, yes."

"Well, in that case, you have to take the money, because if you don't, what you just did up there on that stage would be the absolutely worst birthday present anybody could receive!"

Bastard!

Worse of all, worse than bastard comedians and bastard audiences, must surely be bastard friends.

Chapter 9 - Onward Christian Soldier

I think we can all agree that some gigs however, are just downright weird.

Deal? Yes, we have an agreement, but I mean the town on the south coast of England. It lies on the border of the North Sea and the English Channel and is a former fishing, mining and garrison town.

A garrison town is something to do with troops being stationed there, I believe. And there was a right old trouper at a gig in said town many moons ago. A trouper by the name of Paul Kerensa. And note that I changed *trooper* to *trouper* there, as the first being a soldier and the second an experienced and uncomplaining entertainer. I certainly can't describe Paul as a Stormtrooper because it is safe to say that nobody stormed this show but he was certainly a trouper.

Worry not, all will become clear as to why.

Paul is a completely lovely chap and very funny and clever to boot. He is a 'Christian comedian' that does Christian gigs, which having never done any I assume are shows where people don't swear and curse and say all sorts of moral things to get laughs from the church-goers. He does like a beer however, and is also a self-confessed lover of kebabs. That's much more my kind of religion.

Verily 'tis true that this was possibly the weirdest start to any gig in a pub in this very town.

Myself, Mr Kerensa and a couple of other comedians were booked by a chap by the name of Kieran something. I really can't remember his surname. What I do remember however, is that he tried to start running a number of gigs back in the day, to varying degrees of non-success. I remember his fees were always the weird amount £65 per act. That wasn't too bad given the comedians that tended to work for him were all quite new at the time, but still a weird amount nonetheless.

All paid by cheque too, some of which were apparently rather rubber indeed. I personally never had one bounce, but I heard tell that some did.

So, we all turn up to this pub in Deal on what may have been a Thursday evening for the show. It was so far back I can't remember exactly what day of the week it was. But whatever day of the week it was, I remember us all thinking that the town and the pub were both a lot quieter than they should be.

There was a room off to the side of the pub with a stage and a capacity of somewhere in the region of 100 people. We were a little bit early, so needless to say the room was empty.

Kieran turned up just after us as I recall, and seemed a little concerned that nobody was in the room. Despite no posters and clearly very little promotion.

As the show start time drew closer and closer, Kieran had that look on his face again like he was going to lose more money. As such, that game of comedy cat and mouse began. Comedy cat and mouse being a game which happens more often than it should, between comedians and promoters. It's a kind of unspoken game where the promoter tries to get you to cancel the gig because you don't want to play to very few people.

If the comedian decides not to do the gig, technically they shouldn't get paid.

And obviously comedians don't want to play to 3 people, so they subtly try to convince the promoter to make the decision not to go ahead with the gig but obviously, since it was the promoter's decision to cancel, they still have to pay up the readies.

You see how it works? This happened at pretty much every one of Kieran's shows. And he always lost. Quite often a deal is struck somewhere in the middle with half the agreed fees being paid, but Kieran's communications skills and social ineptitude were matched only by his ability to promote a show.

On this occasion, he decided he wasn't going to pull the show. The difference with this show however was that there was still absolutely nobody in the room about 15 minutes past show start time.So, since he was going to have to pay us anyway, he insisted upon the show going ahead. As such, poor Paul Kerensa had to go on and MC the show, despite nobody being in the audience! That's right, Paul Kerensa compered a show to a room of NO PEOPLE!

Kieran's thinking was that much like when the music starts in a room and people hear it, they will drift in. Therefore, surely if a comedian starts talking, people will come in to see what's going on. Obviously, we thought this was the most ridiculous idea of all time from a complete madman who has no idea about live stand-up...

comedy and clearly he just wanted to make us earn our money. The money he was going to lose whatever happened.

It was truly one of the most bizarre and cringeworthy starts to any show I've ever been to. Admittedly, we could've probably been more supportive and sat right at the front talking to Paul, but that probably would've achieved absolutely nothing, so instead we opted to stand at the back and watch this rather unusual spectacle unfold. It was both hilarious and unsettling at the same time.

But then guess what? Yes! People actually walked in! By the time he'd finished his 15 minutes of MCing at the top of the show, we had eleven people sat watching!

Unbelievable! In truth they turned out to be quite a jolly bunch and we all had a fun show.

We all certainly earned our £65 that night I can tell you, but none as much as trooper Paul did. Still, we all got the same money and that was that.

I love telling other comedians and even muggles the story about how Paul MC'd to nobody, but more how he managed to pull it off in the face of such a ludicrous situation.

Onward Christian soldier!

Chapter 10 - White Bunny

I have to say that quite a lot of the more bizarre things happen off stage, even though they are a result of getting round the world to do things on stage.

One of the more confusing things that has ever happened to me at an overseas festival was probably the third time I went to Melbourne. Very baffling indeed.

You see, back then, before I started to do multiple shows throughout multiple festivals and start to crack the code with regards to being able to make a more few Shekels, managing your limited cash flow situation was problematic. It was always a struggle until you've got your ticket money from the festival pay out, or at least getting some occasional cash on the door to buy grub and booze along the way. Or tucker and grog as those things tend to be referred to in Australia.

As such, one will occasionally take on some other unusual, if rare, employment, shall we say.

Given that it was a midweek in the lead-up to Easter, I was asked by Mel, the producer of our shows at the Elephant and Wheelbarrow venue in Melbourne, if I wanted to make a bit of extra cash by handing out Easter eggs dressed as a giant Easter Bunny in a shopping centre.

That's right folks. Me, dressed as the Easter Bunny handing out little chocolate Easter eggs to children. Lovely, you would've thought. Well, actually, given that it was midweek there were a lot more adults around being greedy for choccies than children.

It turned out that the shopping centre was in Lilydale, which was about fifty minutes on a train from Melbourne city centre, but despite the tedious journey out there on the train from Flinders Street station, I took the job. Firstly because I thought it could be fun, as well as a nice source of material, but even more relevant, it was paying $250 a day for two days rabbiting.

And what the hell, nobody is going to know it's me inside that suit, are they? Which brings us to the actual absurd part of the story.

Enter Lindy from Lilydale.

On the second day, I was approached by a woman on her own. Late 30s, I would say. She stopped to strike up a conversation, whilst munching away on my little chocolate eggs. Get your minds out of the gutter and wait for the punchline!

Henceforth, I regaled her with the story of how I ended up in the fluffy white suit ahead of doing the Melbourne International Comedy Festival and she in turn told me that she was out shopping whilst her husband was at work and her seven-year old daughter was at school.

Both of these people in her life were contributing factors to her, rather sadly, probably not being able to come to my show during the festival. However, she would try to come along if she could somehow find the time.

That being the case, I gave her a flyer. Well, I say a flyer, but given how disorganised and skint I was at the time, it was more of a little business card that was doubling up as a flyer whilst waiting for my printing to arrive. Actually, I'm not sure I even ordered flyers that year. Like I said, cashflow, man.

So, Lindy goes off on her merry way to do some shopping passing by again to say another hello and goodbye before disappearing out of the shopping centre and no doubt, back home.

Two days later, I get a text from a number I don't recognise. But it is signed off, Lindy. Lindy from Lilydale.

Well, perhaps Lindy was going to come to my show after all? Lovely. Turns out my little business card flyers do work after all. Along with standing in a shopping centre handing out confectionery. Big Bunny Promotions!

But alas, after a few back and forth text messages, it became quickly apparent that Lindy wasn't so much interested in Nik Coppin the comedian and his comedy festival show, but more interested in the bunny she'd met at the shopping centre coming round for a bit of rabbit action!

Lindy from Lilydale wanted her own little bit of extra-marital fluff, it seems. Now, I'm not one to shy away from a bit of naughtiness, and once the comedy festival kicks in proper, it's always hard to make 50 minute train journeys out for a bit of bunny shagging.

But more worryingly, it hit me that when I met Lindy, I was handing out little chocolate Easter eggs in a big white furry bunny suit, and whilst during my breaks I would take the giant bunny head off for a bit of a breather, I never did that on the shopping mall floor.

Lindy from Lilydale had never actually seen me out of the bunny costume! She had no idea what I looked like underneath! White furry rabbit, brown baldy man. Couldn't be much more different.

So, as adventurous as I can be at times, I never went out to see Lindy from Lilydale. We could've been shagging like rabbits. Well, like a rabbit. I only had one suit!

But then maybe she had a giant bunny fetish and her own suit? Maybe I would've found myself trussed up in a rabbit-hutch-style dungeon, being fed fresh hay and rabbit mix to keep my energy up for round after round of bunny 'loving'. Perhaps even more bizarrely as her husband watched on? As a bunny himself, or some other giant animal.

I've got to be honest, that's just not my thing, so yep, bottled that one. There is only so far that even I will go. And it's not in a basement with a carrot stuck up my arse an' all.

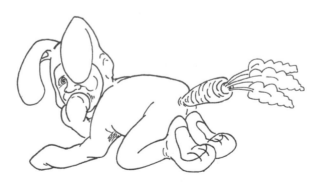

Chapter 11 - Escape From Mornington

Man, sometimes it always pays dividends to take a decision not to make lengthy journeys for a potentially romantic rendezvous. Avoiding the human bunny-boiler was one thing but away from strange encounters in shopping malls, I'm talking about Tinder.

Yes, that infamous shagging, er, I mean dating app that I am glad I no longer have anything to do with. Although, whilst people often refer to it as some kind of shagging app, most women I met on that thing certainly seemed more interested in relationships or friendships. Maybe it's just me?

A few years back in Melbourne, I matched with a woman halfway through the comedy festival. I can't remember her name, probably because I blocked it out of my memory or suppressed the trauma or something, but after a few back and forth messages it came to light that she was looking to date again after her husband passed away six months previously.

That threw up a little red flag, but what the hell, she probably just wanted a bit of company after an emotional few months. Things took an interesting turn when she offered to cover the cost of a taxi out to where she lived. In Mornington! Now, those of you familiar with the geography of the state of Victoria in southern Australia will know it's even further out of the city than Lilydale shopping centre. Quite a bit further.

Out beyond even the badlands of Frankston. That infamous bogan area just on the outskirts of Melbourne.

Still, more often than not being up for a bit of an adventure, I agreed in principle to jump in a taxi after the show one Saturday.

However, given I might have had to get at least the choo-choo to bogan Frankston for the taxi pick-up and I didn't hear back from her until after I had bought some delicious lamb souvlaki (kebab to the Brits) meat from the amazing 24-hour Greek food place in Melbourne known as Stalactites, the deal was off.

And by the way, anyone who's been to the institution that is Stalactites or knows of this place, knows that this food emporium can alone be responsible for you putting on a few kilograms throughout the Melbourne comedy festival. Kilograms that I usually shed cycling and swimming around the Adelaide and Perth Fringes. Well, the cycling tends to take place only in Adelaide where I have a bicycle, but I digress.

So, there I was walking back to my city centre apartment in Melbourne when a call comes through from Mornington lady asking if I'm going to jump in this offered taxi. I told her it was a bit late now and I had bought some food and was heading home. She'd clearly had one or two drinks this Saturday night so her response to this news was to be quite annoyed about my apparent neglect. This was followed by her hanging up the phone.

Another red flag? Probably. I've certainly had my fair share of guilt thrown at me by women in such circumstances and sometimes justifiably, but figured I'd probably had a lucky escape and was more than happy to spend the night with my lamb souvlaki meat and chips. Yum-yum.

A couple of days later, it's our day off from shows. We tend to have Mondays off during the Melbourne comedy festival.

Lo and behold, I get another message from Mornington lady apologising for her behaviour over the phone on Saturday night and inviting me to come across that evening. I was actually hanging out with a couple of buddies in the St Kilda area of Melbourne at the time, which is out in that direction anyway, but it was still a right old trek.

Again she offered to pay for a taxi. Desperate much? Another red flag? I mean, I'm not exactly Brad Pitt! So I'm deliberating whether to go or not. It's not like I'm desperate for a shag or anything, but we had no plans that evening, so maybe. Can I be bothered? She seems keen and rather amusing if nothing else, so maybe. Then to help make up my mind, she sends a rather surprising and completely unsolicited photo of her boobs!

Right, where's the taxi?!

It's booked and on my way to Mornington I go! I think it was a good fifty minutes in the car, if not more, and of course being the all-round good baldy egg that I am, I stopped off to get a bottle of red wine for meself and a cheeky bottle of white wine for the lady.

She said she'd meet me the other end to give the taxi driver the cash, and she was true to her word. She's waiting just down the road from her house and pays the $107 taxi fare! ONE HUNDRED AND SEVEN DOLLARS! I mean that's probably only a couple of quid in real British money, but blimey!

But here's the thing. She's pissed. As a fart! Drunk as a skunk, man! I mean, you know when you can smell the booze on someone's breath after a few beers, wines or spirits? Well, not that. It's like the alcohol is oozing from every part of her body. Like even her bones were saturated with the stuff. Add to that the fags. She absolutely reeked of cigarette smoke.

I immediately feel like I may have made a boo-boo here but she seems pleasant enough and I certainly don't want to be lumbered with a $100+ taxi fare and another one back should I decide to abandon this 'date' immediately, so I decided to see how the rendezvous played out. What harm can she be? She's sweet in nature and a diminutive 4ft 10in tall and very slight of build. She looks a bit bumblebee-like with the way her blonde hair was styled, large-ish eyes and head that appeared slightly more largely out of proportion with her tiny body frame, but you know, bumblebees can be cute. Until they sting you! But she might be quite funny and have some good DVD's back home. She clearly just wanted some company, so it could be a laugh.

We wandered to her abode and in we went. Her house was on three levels. An immediate small flight of stairs up to the kitchen area and out to the garden, then round to the right again, takes one up to the huge living room area and to the right again, up to the two bedrooms and bathroom area. All quite relevant to the story.

No sooner are we in the place than she's gone straight for the garden to smoke more cigarettes. I did get offered some wine on the way through, mind. And of course, I put the bottle of white

I'd bought in her fridge too. Keep that shit cool, man. After three or four fags and some gazing at the starry sky and I'm led up to the spacious living room area, which has a very comfortable sofa and the biggest TV screen I'd seen in ages. Things are looking up for some boozy movie viewing at least! That'll do me for the evening, I thought, even if she drinks and smokes herself into a coma.

But first I had to make a call to my bank in the UK. A credit card payment has taken place that I'm not sure about, so whilst I did that, she went off for another ciggie in the garden. Of course she did. The payment was to update my mailing list provider, so all good. I'd changed it over from my debit card and forgotten about it.

But as I'm waiting to hear this from the bank person over the phone, Mornington woman returns to the living room and starts virtually molesting me! I had to get her to stop so I could finish my call and eventually she does and goes off for... yes, another smoke.

So the call ended and I sat down on what is quite possibly the most comfortable sofa I have ever sat on, EVER, and then she appeared back from downstairs and sits beside me. I start talking to her about life and what's happened and I think I got about two minutes in before she's jumped on top of me and started kissing me. Sixty seconds later and she's completely naked! Right on top of me. I can barely move. She was absolutely stinking of cigarettes and alcohol and she had to be the worst kisser of all time. And that's taking into account one of my mates' slobberchops of a dog that is far too affectionate for one so salivary.

It was the worst, man! Ever!

Then she rolled off me and into the sofa legs akimbo to further the 'action'. But as she does so, from actions of which I'm still shell-shocked about, she reveals a backside that - and I hate to be so graphic - looks like it's recently done a 'number two' and the owner of said backside hasn't bothered to wash or wipe. Too drunk to remember basic hygiene, I reckon. Anyway, that's the absolute deal breaker for me. I mean, I couldn't go through with this anyway, even with a clean well-wiped botty. She was too drunk and clearly too emotionally-charged to be making any rational decisions of an intimate nature. Shagging drunk women is not my thing. On many an occasion, orders to imbibe some water or other sobering beverage have had to be issued in the past, when affairs of a carnal nature are on the table.

After all, consent is fundamental. Just ask James Nokise. Not that you have to ask, he'll tell you anyway. Again and again and again.

She sensed my reluctance and started to go ballistic, screaming about how I don't want her and she's unattractive and all sorts like that. I've been there before and it's not pleasant or fair. But this is a different kettle of sea-dwelling scaly creatures.

Then she jumped up and ran downstairs almost in tears. For yes, more cigarettes in the garden.

That's it, I think. I need to go! But how do I go? I don't really know where I am! Not in the big scheme of things anyway.

Can I get a train? A bus? Probably not.

I know a taxi is expensive. So out comes the iPhone! And it reveals that there are still trains from the badlands of Frankston station! Maybe I can get a taxi there?

I also try contacting my mate Noel who lives in Elsternwick which is kind of out in that direction from Melbourne as well in the hope he can drive down and carry me away in his motor, but he is incapacitated by way of being drunk himself and can't make it. Noel is a rather interesting character in himself, so stay tuned for more on him.

But before I can make my next move, she was back! She runs straight past me and up the next flight of stairs into bedroom and throws herself under the covers, whining and moaning in her inebriated state. I went in to see if she's okay and she's crying saying that she's ugly and horrible and that nobody has wanted her since her husband died and she might as well just kill herself and that I should just leave if I don't want her.

That was my plan to be honest, but now I'm getting this suicidal guilt trip?!

I wanted to tell her that it's nothing to do with her looks, but more the fact she smokes like a chimney and drinks like a fish. Not that fish drink alcohol of course, but you get my point. However, not being a counsellor, I don't feel it's my place to offer such advice and it might only make her worse at a time like this. Especially since both things appear to be emotional crutches upon which she is clearly leaning.

So I try to calm her down and after about 10 minutes it appeared to be working and she tells me if I want to stay despite not wanting to have sex with her, there is the spare room. However, given her erratic actions and alcoholism, I don't fancy the idea of possibly waking up in the afterlife with scissors sticking out of my head, so I'm about to make my excuses when she jumps out of bed and runs back to the garden for yet another cigarette.

This is my last chance, I think. As soon as she disappeared into the garden, I quickly ran down the stairs. I got down to the first landing, from my earlier explanation of the layout of the house. The door is in sight and all I've got to do is get down one more small flight of stairs then out to freedom. But as anybody knows, you never leave a good man behind. And in that fridge was a lovely chilling bottle of white wine.

In order to liberate that white wine though, I've got to head towards the garden where the potential murderous woman lies in wait. But I have to do it! I have to!
So I do! I stealthily creep into the kitchen, open the fridge door, grab the wine, throw it into my bag and creep back down that flight of stairs to the front door. I quietly opened the door, stepped outside, closed the door and then ran like Ben Johnson on his steroids.

Anyone that hasn't seen that infamous 100m sprint final at the 1988 Seoul Olympics has to check it out, by the way. Canadian Ben Johnson, muscles bulging like the Incredible Hulk crosses the finish line metaphorical miles ahead of Carl Lewis and our own Linford Christie with a hand in the air and the coolness of somebody reading the Sunday papers. He might as well have been wearing a T-shirt reading, "I'm On Steroids".

So, I'm out! The first establishment I see is a place called the Kirk Hotel. I try the main door and it's locked! It's only like 8:30pm for crying out loud! Mornington! I do know from previous experience of road trips between Adelaide and Melbourne in the past that a lot of these small coastal towns in Australia close down quite early. Damn! I can just see in my mind's eye, crazy lady catching up with me, like a scene from Wolf Creek or something. What can I do?

I walked round to the side of the building and luckily I found a side door open! And there is somebody at a bar! I asked if they could call me a taxi and they did.
The taxi arrived about 15 minutes later and I jumped in, glad to still be alive, and it drives me to the bogan badlands of Frankston. I have to be honest, despite everything that I've heard about the place and it's never good I can assure you, Frankston was like a paradise! I was so glad to be there.

I had just missed a train and the next one was in 20 minutes. Fortunately, there were people at the station in case of a late attack from a mad person, potentially in deadly pursuit. I've never been so happy to be on a train finally leaving a station. That was possibly the longest 20 minutes of my life, which was only to be superseded by the amount of time I almost did on stage in Torremolinos in the May of 2018. Still imagining that the lights on the train would start to flicker and I would see a diminutive figure with a blade in hand coming through the communicating carriage doors, I breathed a sigh of relief.

Then the phone rang! It's her! I let it go to voicemail, only to listen to the message when I finally arrived back in the safe, comforting, soothing arms of Melbourne city centre.

"You left," the voice said, in the sweetest of soft tones, "You didn't even say goodbye..." As I listened, a slight feeling of sympathy came over me and maybe a pang of sorrow, but then the voice deepened and became louder and rather sinister, almost Disney movie witch-like. "You're weak! You're a weak man, Nik. WEAK AS PISS!"

Maybe. Maybe I am. And whilst I'm not one to scare easily or run away at 100mph from a lady meeting, I'm still alive, I didn't end up shagging her shitty bum-hole and I don't have scissors sticking out of my head.

Chapter 12 - Tarantula

I've said it before and I'll it again, you can't trust comedians.

Even the ones that will fly you over to Cambodia to headline a show in the capital city of Phnom Penh.

On this occasion, I'm talking about comedian and promoter Dan Riley. Now, when you first meet him, you might think he's a lovely guy that has your best interests at heart. And why wouldn't he, if he's going to get you over to close his show? Well, let me explain.

Thoroughly looking forward to my tour of Dubai, Singapore, Vietnam and Cambodia I was, until tragedy struck.

And what a tragic situation it turned out to be. I mean you wouldn't expect to be forced by said comedian/promoter, as well as other British and American comedians on the bill to eat a giant spider. Of course you wouldn't. Why would you? Who would even think such a thing?

However, perhaps I have myself to blame, given that upon being met at the airport by Mr Dan and jumping in a tuk-tuk, I commented on the fact that I had seen video footage of market places in Phnom Penh that have bucket loads of tarantulas that they had captured in the jungles which they fry up and eat.

"Sure," he replies. They are considered a delicacy here in Cambodia. People often eat spiders and rice. Wait, did he just say, 'spiders and rice'? I mean, we've all heard of chicken and rice. I certainly have, especially with my father being from the

Caribbean island of Barbados where that dish is seen as a delicacy.

And of course, we've all heard of having pilau rice with your lamb shashlik in an Indian restaurant after a few Cobras. The brand of beer that is, not the actual deadly snake. But 'spiders and rice'? Who has ever heard of such a thing? And who in their right mind would consider it a delicacy?!

People in Cambodia it seems. Apparently it became a thing after the Khmer Rouge forced thousands of people to leave the cities and survive out in the wild.

Mr Dan goes on to say, "In fact, there's a market place en route to where you are staying that cooks and sells tarantulas. If you like, we can stop by and get some."

Of course, not wanting to sound like some wussy-wuss, I'm like, "Yeah, sure, why not?" God damn the patriarchy. However, we arrived just as the woman was packing up her outdoor kitchen after selling out of her spidery wares.

How thoroughly unfortunate.

So, after a bit of a chill out beside the pool at my hotel and being met again by Mr Dan, let's cut forward to the gig that evening. And even further forward to after my 30 minute set which I thought went reasonably well. I even made reference to being a superhero fan and more especially the Spider-Man image on my T-shirt. Because let's face it, if you are wearing a T-shirt with the image of the greatest superhero ever on it, it must be mentioned.

It should also be noted that whilst I am a Spider-Man fan, I am absolutely not, repeat, absolutely not, a fan of spiders themselves. Some might say that that doesn't really make sense, but to me, it's perfect, given that arachnophobia is arguably the world's biggest phobia and Spider-Man is (not) arguably the world's most popular superhero.

Still confused? Well then let me explain. One therapy with regards to getting over a fear of something is to face up to it and see it in a good light. Therefore, the fact that Spider-Man is a hero means that subconsciously children like him because in an albeit obscure way, it is looking at spiders in a positive way.

Something for people who understand such matters to discuss further. So, back to my tail of eight-legged woe.

The mention of said superhero of course, gives the MC - on the scurrilous instructions of said promoter Mr Dan - a good lead-in to get me back on stage where I am presented with two tarantulas in a plastic bag. Massive black ones. Now I've been given some gifts after comedy shows in the past, but I'm not sure I've had any quite potentially vomit-inducing as dead fried tarantulas. What a treat!

Oh, but the situation goes from bad present to a much more daunting scenario as Glaswegian MC Steven Halcrow and Liverpudlian support act, Scotty Muldoon along with an audience much akin to those in the Coliseums in ancient Rome baying for blood, begin a joint campaign for me to eat said tarantulas before their very eyes.

If you can't trust comedians, you can certainly trust Glaswegians and Scouse ones even less!

A initial call from the Scouser of "Shall we get him to eat the spiders?" starts off proceedings and loud cries of "SPIDER! SPIDER! SPIDER! SPIDER!" ring out around the room.

Not quite feeling as exulted as possibly the amazing Spider-Man himself would do after saving a child from getting hit by a juggernaut, I tentatively suggest that I will only do it if a member of the audience does it as well. By this, I specifically mean the English girl in the front row who everybody has had banter with throughout the night. She is wearing those ridiculous elephant image travel pants after all.

Why do so many people wear those things?

Of course we didn't get said English lady on stage in the end, because again, you can't trust comedians. And way, way worse than Glaswegian and Scouse ones, are probably American ones. Especially when they are new American comedians that don't understand the true magic of theatre and they charge to the front of the room towards the stage shouting at the top of their annoying American voice,
"I'LL DO IT!".

Brilliant. So now not only have I got to eat at least some part of this hideous spider in a plastic bag, I don't even get to do it with a nice English travelling lady, but instead a very annoying Yank. An annoying yank in a polo T-shirt, shorts with pockets that are way too big for him, brown lace-up shoes and socks virtually up to his knees. Oh Joy!

The chants of SPIDER! SPIDER! SPIDER! SPIDER!" continue
as I take a little bite of a tarantula leg. To be fair, so does Scouse
Scotty Muldoon, even though he's actually a vegetarian. The
cheeky bastard is leading the chanting after all.
The Glaswegian joins in and they insist that I take another bite.

I just about managed to get another bite without throwing up
all over the stage as I can feel the crispy hairy tarantula leg
crunching between my molars. The situation is exacerbated by
the annoying Yank who grabs the rest of the arachnid and
throws it all in his big mouth, chews it and swallows it.
Cephalothorax, pedipalps, abdomen, remaining legs, the lot.
Truly disgusting. But what does one expect from those lot from

over the pond? Still, if one considers that to be a victory for an American over a Brit, I'm happy to lose that particular contest.

So, heaving and coughing and feeling a little bit of cooked tarantula hair still between my teeth, I make my way to the bar where I insist upon some beers. And of course, Mr Dan, you are going to buy them for me!

Chowing down on the legs of a tarantula in Phnom Penh, Cambodia!

Chapter 13 - Asian Hulk

Right, so when I say 'Asian Hulk'. I am not referring to that ridiculous Amadeus Cho Korean Hulk nonsense. There is only one true Hulk and that's Bruce Banner. Almost as bad as the Miles Morales version of Spider-Man. We are talking Hulks of a different kind. Keep your peepers reading on and all will become clear.

Without doubt, some of the best shows and times I've had are at venues and places in Southeast Asia.

Such a marvellous part of the world.

As with most things in life, you have to take the good with the bad, the rough with the smooth. After all, it's not always great comedy shows with beer and tasty Asian food thereafter, sometimes you're force-fed large black hideous fried tarantulas by unscrupulous show promoters and comedians, who will use ones arachnophobia against them. So mean. But even then, there are more scary things than being made to eat dead fried spiders, no matter how big they may be.

For shows and for jollies, one of the best places to visit in the Southeast Asia region, is Thailand. Arguably one of the best places to visit on the entire planet actually.

A delightful juxtaposition of beauty, culture and of course great fun getting lashed up at late bars. Patong, in Phuket, being one of the best places to do such a thing. Pattaya - should you like that sort of thing is another one of these places - but it is a bit bigger than Patong and a bit too crazy if you ask me.

Horrible stinky beach as well with too many overly tanned expats. The bit I was in anyway.

Still, after a night of getting my arse kicked at Connect 4 and games of pool by the women and lady boys working in the bars and having to buy them drinks for the privilege, one likes to partake in some of the delicious late night street food. And more especially, fried chicken! Apologies for maintaining the stereotype, brothers and people who suffer from white guilt who would rather such things went unsaid, but that shit is good, man. So is watermelon.

On this one occasion, I approached one of my favourite late-night street food vendors on Bangla Road in Patong for some of the best fried chicken at about 3am. I'm a bit... 'merry', shall we say. I'm waiting for said poultry to be heated up when two rather diminutive and pretty young Thai women also approached the food station.

They are talking and giggling amongst themselves and I notice that one of them kind of surreptitiously points towards me mid-sentence.

I've had this happen before, of course. On rare occasions it's because somebody has recognised me from a comedy show. As I say, rare occasions. More often however, it happens to be somebody noticing whatever superhero I happen to be sporting on my T-shirt that day. They might be a fan of that superhero in particular, or Marvel or DC in general.

Of course, anybody that prefers DC to Marvel is, well, wrong.

But it's always nice to find a fellow superhero fan. Not just because it's good to have a conversation about all things super-hero, but people can often surprise us. To digress slightly, I'll give you one example in particular. One that I was slightly ashamed and embarrassed by, as it happens.

I was walking through the main shopping area in the centre of Perth in Western Australia one sunny afternoon before the Fringe World shows that evening and I notice a chap staggering towards me, clearly focused on striking up some kind of conver-sation. In those circumstances the conversation usually centres around said person wanting money or a cigarette or such like. As a non-smoker, and sadly in the middle of a fringe festival, I usually have neither on me.

So, I'd rather not engage in such a conversation given that an inebriated person can sometimes take offence thinking you are brushing them off in some kind of superior act of dismissive-ness. And who can blame an Aboriginal in Australia given how history has treated their people?

Aboriginals often refer to me as 'brother' too, given that I have occasionally been mistaken for one myself and this chap is no different as he puts his hand out towards me, but rather than going for a handshake or a fist pump, he points at my T-shirt and says in and intoxicated voice, "The Silver Surfer!"

Who would've thought that an aboriginal bloke not com-pletely in control of his faculties through alcohol consumption would even know, let alone recognise the Silver Surfer?! As bril-liant and interesting a character as the 'Sky Rider of the

Spaceways' is, as well as being extremely powerful, would easily beat Superman in a fight (had to get that DC dig in there), as well as probably being my third favourite superhero behind Spider-Man and the Hulk, he is not generally recognised. And he has often been mistaken for Iceman. Who let's face it, is way more shit. Don't be giving me the cold shoulder now X-Men fans, because he is. Certainly compared to the Silver Surfer.

A great example of a person surprising me with their insight, but also how we all can, and often do, have preconceived notions and ideas about what people are like before even talking to them. He was a top bloke and I wish I'd had time to engage him in more conversation about superheroes.

Back to the Thai girls. On this day I had the aforementioned second favourite superhero of mine, the Incredible Hulk on my T-shirt. So, given that they definitely haven't recognised me from a comedy show, I assume they are pointing towards the not-so-jolly green giant on my chest.

So, I look towards them, smile and say, "Yes, the Hulk."

Then, the girl closest to me laughs and says, "No, I was pointing at you because my friend was going to order lots of food and I said to her that if she orders too much, she will get fat like you!"

For fuck's sake, man! Just how direct are these Thai girls? I mean, you didn't have to be quite so honest, especially given that if I had maybe overheard her discussing my figure (or lack thereof), I had already given her a get-out by making it about the Hulk!

But no! She made it quite clear that they were laughing at my portliness.

To be fair, I do overindulge sometimes. Lots of times.

That is not the only time I've had a less than savoury encounter on Bangla Road in Patong, however.

There was this one time that a very tall (even if you took away the high heels) lady boy, or 'kathoey', if you want to give her the proper politically correct term, as I believe it to be. However, despite what the PC brigade say, most people in Thailand, like this lady, seem more than happy with the term 'lady boy' and generally refer to themselves as such and actually have a very good line in self-deprecating comedy.

I had seen this particular lady on a number of occasions, on this and previous trips, and she was always quite straightforward and dare I say it, slightly aggressive in wanting, from what I could see (from a reasonable distance), as money for sex.

Fortunately, I had always passed by unnoticed.

Until this one such occasion, when she decided to stomp on up to me in her high heels, tight jeans and low-cut top. She wasn't unattractive by any means, but unlike some of the more demure lady-like lady boys, it was not only very obvious that she was a kathoey, but she probably had a couple of inches on me, and her shoulders were just as wide. She was relatively large, but also very athletic. Not a chubster, as previously pointed out by the girls laughing at me at the chicken stand.

She made it quite clear she was touting for business of a carnal nature. As always, despite being happy to have a laugh,

I was not interested in such activities. But given it was late and she was usually quite aggressive anyway, she elected to get angry with me for denying her the chance to make a few Thai baht, and so ripped the baseball cap off my noggin and demanded money for it to be returned to my personage. 200 baht she wanted, which equates to approximately five British pounds... FIVE QUID?!

That's at least a couple of beers in Thailand!

How dare she steal my baseball cap and then demand that I have to give her some of my hard-earned cash to get my own headgear back?!

She was right up in my grill and properly squaring up to me, so given I am one who believes in equality and equal rights, and who believes in not just those things but that theft is completely wrong, I looked straight back in her eye and made it clear that I was livid and she was not getting any money out of me.

This just made her more abusive and aggressive and she was clearly fully prepared to take this to fisticuffs.

So, I looked at her shoulders, her muscular athletic build, the high-heel stilettos and long, sharp fingernails and realised with that build, those shoes and the nails, it would've been like fighting the Black Widow, Deathstrike and She-Hulk all rolled into one person!

Therefore, I had no choice but to deal with this situation as any red-blooded male with self-respect and a sense of right and wrong would do...

I ran off and let her keep the fucking thing!

"If you want your cap, come and get it!"

Chapter 14 - Comedy Can Be Draining

Kuala Lumpur is the place in Asia I have probably most frequented, with maybe the exception of Singapore. Upon my second visit I think, a newish act by the name of Chrissy Wu suggested I do a show on the island of Penang.

Penang is to the north-west of mainland Malaysia, about an hour on a plane or a few hours drive or on the bus.

"Lovely food". That's what everybody always says whenever you mention Penang. Well, in Malaysia and other parts of Asia at least. The ignorant westerners like myself would probably have no idea.

Everybody always said it. And to be fair, it's true. I did frequent some rather nice eateries on the island. Certainly in the capital, George Town. I saw and ate blue rice for the first time! Blue rice! Batu Feringghi, where I've also stayed for a bit had some pretty nice food too, but George Town had it beat. Batu is more beachy and touristy in that way a place can be, so it's a lot more cultured in George Town too. It's very arty, lots of nice little coffee shops and funny little museums. They are just tourist attractions really, but museums sounds better, I guess.

I mean, they have a 'Ghost Museum' for instance. How can you have a museum for something that doesn't exist and never has?! No matter what that fraud Derek Accorah said, there are no such things as ghosts! However, the Upside-Down Museum was rather fun.

A 'museum' of upside-down things no less. You basically have your photo taken with bits of furniture and the like stuck to the ceiling.

Fun topsy-turvy times. And when you see the photos you do feel rather Spider-Man like. Yep, got another reference in there!

Becoming Spider-Man

Anyway, lovely place Penang and I met some lovely people doing a couple of shows at a venue called Kim Haus. It's a hotel with a performance bar in it which used to be a place that made its own gold jewellery. They still have a lot of the equipment there which is quite interesting. A very cool boutique hotel indeed. Charming and delightful, whereas most boutique hotels I've stayed in just seem to be shabby places with a cheap arty design or theme and called 'boutique' to paper over the cracks of their shitness and up the price. Wow, I'm really getting cynical in my old age. Still, doesn't mean I'm not right.

Lusy, who attended both the shows I did at Kim Haus with friends, was the main instigator of getting me back over to the island to do a preview of my developing show (at the time) 'Shark'. That, as well as me hosting some workshops and show-cases with some aspiring new comedians. Lusy is an art teacher who runs a thing called Little Art House Studios, which puts on a number of different events with artistic merit.

Up until this point, the only stand-up comedian in Penang was a chap by the name of 'Garu'. If my memory serves me correctly, at the time of our first meeting he'd been doing stand-up for about a year or so, in his late twenties and was quite shy and unassuming upon introduction. However, he certainly came out of his shell and didn't mind taking the piss out of more 'established' comedians on stage.

Something I thought was quite cheeky but very ballsy. But I liked the kid. I liked his shy off-stage, yet cheeky demeanour on-stage, as well as the fact that he wore a black suit with white Michael Jackson-esque gloves was rather interesting and appealing to me. He also used to do a joke about a water cooler bottle too, so had to carry it around with him to and from the gig. A full water cooler bottle.
Bloody heavy things, they are. He brought it to an eatery one night after a show too, which was odd, but I found it curious and entertaining.

Six months after I'd done the very first comedy workshops with him - and some others that wanted to try stand-up - I re-turned to the burgeoning comedy scene in Penang. At that time, pretty much all of the people that did my workshops and the

Cheeky wee shite, Garu!

showcase had been doing quite a few open spots around the place. I like to think I had a big hand in helping the comedy scene to grow on the island and that makes me happy. They are all amazing people.

So, it was decided that we should put on a showcase with me as MC and them doing 5 - 10 minute sets with me giving them feedback afterwards. And I have to say, they had come along rather spiffingly. They must've had a good tutor.

The showcase was held at a place called 'That Little Wine

Bar' in an area that I probably wouldn't be able to pronounce even if I could remember it. Tommes, a German bloke who was at my workshop owns the bar which was very handy indeed for what turned out to be Penang's first ever all-comedy open mic showcase. Makes me proud to be involved, I tells ya!

Tommes runs this bar across from what looks to me to be a rather sizeable a nice house that he indeed, owns. Apparently the result of many things he has worked on in the past, but most notably him being a celebrity chef in Asia for a couple of years. He likes to consider himself the German Gordon Ramsey of Asia, but I made it quite clear he will be referred to as the German Jamie Oliver of Asia.

Sorry, my German bud, we all have to deal with the piss-taking from time-to-time.

For example, like with regard to that cheeky wee shite Garu closing the showcase with this opening gambit:

"Hello everyone. Yeah… I used to be able to say I'm the only stand-up comedian in Penang. But now you can see we have a few more. So these days I say I'm the most experienced comedian in Penang. But of course, that's until Nik Coppin comes to town. In which case I say I'm the funniest comedian in Penang!" Brazen wee fucker! And of course, the audience lap that shit up! Bastards!

After the showcase, I was offered by Lusy's boyfriend and soon-to-be baby's father, Watson - who was also one of the performers at the workshop and showcase - a lift back to George Town, where he was dropping off Juliana Heng, the opening act at the showcase who not only came all the way up from Kuala Lumpur to attend, but also remembered me from the workshops I did back down there in the capital. She was pretty aces on stage too.

Watson thought that despite me staying in the spare room of the apartment he shared with Lusy, I might quite like to hang out at 'Love Lane', which is Penang's crazy street. Where all the Indians and Malaysians like to go to try their luck at pulling a white backpacker girl out on the lash spending daddies money. That sort of place. Great people-watching fodder is Love Lane.

And as it so happens, over yonder from where I was staying with Lusy and Watson in Penang, I could see 'Jerejak Island'.

A former penal colony.

Yep, Malaysia has Jerejak, America has Alcatraz, but us Brits have got....

....AUSTRALIA!

Now, where have I heard that before? Far too many times? Hmmm, I wonder.

Anyway, so Love Lane also has one of the best burger stands I have ever been to; 'Old Trafford Burger'. Yep, a late night burger stand in Penang, Malaysia, named after the Manchester United stadium. It has the Red Devil badge logo thing on the stand and everything. There was a time that I, as an Arsenal fan, would've been disgusted buying a burger from this late night place but the burgers are absolutely delicious, so it has to be done. However, nowadays, I'm more ashamed and embarrassed that people might mistakenly think it's because I'm a Man Utd fan!

Anyway, I decided that I would leave my people-watching for that night and to get a couple of beers at the 7-Eleven which is 20 minutes walk from Lusy and Watson's apartment. "You just drop me at the shop and off you go back to be with Lusy. I'm fine walking back," I tell him. "I want to check out the area and I think I need the exercise."

So off drives Watson leaving me to purchase my very reasonably priced cans of Carlsberg lager and thereafter off I go on my stroll back to the apartment. My iPhone apps had been playing up most of the day, but I managed to get Google maps to give me directions back to their apartment and on the way back, of course, I want to message my lovely girlfriend back home. I am missing her after all, what with me being the old romantic that I am.

Now rather than do the thumbs thing, I always like to use the dictation thing on the iPhone keyboard. Very handy bit of kit that. Even though it freaks people out wondering why I am talking to my phone in such a fashion. You talk the message and it writes it out for you. What is so hard to understand? Yet people often react like it's witchcraft.

So, as I'm doing my dictation with my iPhone screen up to my face, I decide to walk along the darkened path just outside the houses alongside the dual carriageway, and as such, I veer off in that direction. Then, as I'm halfway through a message about a previously discussed scenic Sunday afternoon walk from Brighton to Rottingdean for a pub lunch, my foot seems to give way.

The next thing I know, my bag is off my back, my phone and some contents of my bag along with my money and myself have crashed down at the bottom of a four-foot drainage ditch!

"Fucking hell!" is the only thing I can think to say, as I peel my items out of the ditch and place them on the sidewalk. I go about clambering out of said drainage ditch, blood all down my knees, toes and arms and check for any serious damage.

Fortunately it seems my toe isn't broken and I can still hobble my way back to the apartment despite my bad knee, which was the subject of a cartilage operation years ago, having taken a serious knock.

But alas in all of the commotion of me taking a fall into the ditch and climbing back out, my iPhone, which is still having problems, has lost the directions back to the apartment. I thought I should get a few snaps of my injuries for social media (not for a doctor, that would be silly) and in doing so, lost my map and subsequent route home with my phone playing silly buggers. After I hobble and wander around for a good 45 minutes trying to remember how to get to a place I've only been once thus far, feeling sorry for myself and wondering where I'm going to sleep and how I'm going to get in touch with anybody at all with my problematic phone, I somehow manage to get my apps working again!

Hallelujah! Lord be praised! Even though I don't believe in all of that tomfoolery.

Of course, this was only the second night I had stayed in the apartment - which is why I didn't know my way back - so given it was a secure condominium, the security guard looked at this dark-skinned English bloke hobbling towards them in a brightly coloured baseball cap and T-shirt, with shorts and flip-flops and blood dripping from his hands, arms and legs, and decided I was not a trustworthy sight. So cynical! As such they really put me through the security ringer, and finally after proving myself genuine, with the help of previous messages from Lusy, a guard escorts me to their flat to make sure my key actually works and I'm not some robber or murderer.

Thereupon I clean up my wounds and administer some Band-Aids that I luckily had the presence of mind to bring with me. I was a Cub Scout after all. "Akela, we will do our best," and be prepared and all that business.

So, despite my job taking me all over the world, trust me when I tell you, being an international travelling comedian can be quite draining.

As in, you know, I fell into a drain? A pun on comedy being tiring and me falling into a four-foot drainage ditch. Oh, just forget it.

Chapter 15 - The Killer In Manila

I have to say that in all the places I've been around the world to do comedy shows, Manila in the Philippines is probably the one I'm least likely to want to go back to.

Well, there and the Tottenham area in North London. And not just because I am an Arsenal fan. I'm not stupid enough to wear a Gunners shirt walking around the place. It's just, well, a bit shit.

There is an air of lawlessness about Manila, and you always feel you have to have your guard up and be looking over your shoulder. I'm not one to scare easily, except when approached by athletic, aggressive lady-boys in high heels of course, but there is a palpable feeling of murderousness about the place.

The one and only show I actually performed there was actually my Shaggers show. I did watch some other shows, which were awful enough in themselves but Shaggers took the biscuit. And by that I mean it was probably the worst Shaggers show I've had to perform at. Shaggers, if I've not said previously, being a line-up show with comedians doing material all based around sex and relationships gone wrong.

Shaggers, as well as my solo show and many other shows had done a tour of Hong Kong and Singapore, as part of the Magner's International Comedy Festival.
It was the second time out for this tour, the first of which was only over a few days in Singapore.

Jolly nice time that was too where I made some great friends. And whilst the second tour was fun in a loopy-group-of-comedians-on-tour type of way, it had its issues. Included in there was a lovely two day holiday in Puerta Galera in the Philippines, an extremely delightful trip, it has to be said… before heading to crazy Manila.

The Shaggers show in Manila was for some reason organised as part of an expat ladies night in a bar. A show where a variety of comedians talk about sex and relationships in a packed room surrounded by drunken women who couldn't give a shit about comedy. Brilliant. Most times you can play the male and female card and question people about their relationships and their sex lives, but when you have one hundred extremely inebriated ex-pat women in a room, it would be less painful to dig your own eyes out with a spatula.

'Hell on toast' is the expression I usually use for such gigs.

It's not often that I am pleased for one of my own shows, and especially Shaggers to be over, but fuck me, I couldn't leave fast enough.

After the show, I met up with Alex Petty, who I often produce shows with, and a lovely English/Irish/Colombian comedian by the name of Matthew Giffen. Well, like me, he's as English as they come, but given his mixed heritage, he likes to play that Irish potatoes and Colombian cocaine card on stage, and all to hilarious affect, I should add.

Nice chap who often had to carry a bag of potatoes around with him as a prop for his shows. One of the best things I think

Matthew, Alex and I did on this particular trip was to crash numerous wedding photos in a large park in Hong Kong holding up his bag of potatoes to be snapped.

To be honest, I think the wedding couples and their parties were more than happy to have a bunch of potato-wielding comedians in their posh pretentious overly-expensive photographs. Something different, a little bit unusual and a mad story to tell the grandchildren, I suppose.

Anyway, myself, Matthew and Alex decided to wind down with a couple of drinks at a bar away from the plastered women baying for blood, cock or both.

However, in true Manila style, things can go from bad to worse in an instant. On this occasion, the three of us (as the known part-organisers at this shoddily-but-amusingly-put-together festival) were called across to one of the other venues by what I can only describe as a rather distressed and panicking young Filipino chap acting as one of a number of our local show managers.

We sauntered over to find out why he appeared to be in such an anguished state. As if just being in Manila isn't enough of a reason.

He told us that he was quite in fear of the currently performing comedian's life. Now I'm not one to accuse anybody of overreacting - well, actually I am - but this did seem a bit of an overstatement. I mean, we've all heard of comedians dying on stage but not actually being murdered whilst plying their trade.

However, as he is telling us the story, there was also a leather biker jacket-clad British expat Liverpudlian in his late 50's, sat ten feet away on a chair outside the bar going absolutely Garrity about something or other. Based upon our Filipino show manager's story, we ascertain that apparently the comedian on stage, Eleanor Tiernan - who is a very funny and more importantly, very lovely, Irish woman - had seriously disrespected this Scouser's Filipino wife.

Apparently, due to yet another mad audience (including this expat), as well as various games of whatever playing on the huge televisions around the sports bar, Eleanor's solo show wasn't going very well, to say the least. As such, said Filipino wife took it upon herself to deliver a shot of vodka to the stage.

Eleanor, not wishing to divulge the reason she didn't want the vodka as a recovering alcoholic, repeatedly refused the offering. Despite this, the drink was forced into her hand and Eleanor thought she could do nothing else but make a point that she really didn't like it by pouring the vodka onto the stage.

Of course, this is the story told by the Scouse bloke who was pretty blotto.

However, it comes to light that within this sports bar, outback, there was a massive biker club of which he is a member and he's making all sorts of threats about what might happen to the comedian lady on stage as well as any of her friends, should she not apologise to his wife. 20 years they've been married and nobody has been so disrespectful to her in all this time, he also tells us. Says the man threatening to kill a nice Irish lady on stage.

We are trying to calm the situation down when he disappears inside the bar and when he returns he has a biker buddy with him.

Well, I say 'biker buddy', but that sounds all-too-friendly an appearance for somebody who seriously looks like a cross between Fu Manchu and Lobo from the DC comics universe! Anybody who knows either of these two characters will know that it would be easy to imagine this man cutting us all into small pieces and feeding us to some hogs.

Needless to say, we start to poop our panties but do our best to remain calm and explain the situation to Lobo Manchu, as he nods his head appearing to understand.

However, fortunately for the three of us and our even more scared-shitless show manager, he turns out to be a very amiable and rather decent chap. It also turns out that he thinks that this raging Liverpudlian, whom he knows from the club is also a bit of a bellend.

Result! Thanks Lobo Manchu.

Still, while he and the mad northern Englishman are discussing said situation, myself, Alex and Matthew quickly dive inside the bar, and give Eleanor the signal with the eyes to get off stage immediately. Fortunately, she took her cue, jumped off the stage and followed us as we scuttled out of the back alley of the pub.

A good few drinks were had that night, I can assure you. Back at the hotel and another bar down the road, as we regale our fellow tour comrades with the story of potentially ending up in a box.

I believe my two partners, in what could've been a biker-induced Manila murder, went off with a large party of people, who were also on our Asian tour, to watch to watch some dwarves boxing that night. Not having gone myself, and never actually having been to such an event, I sadly can't tell you anything about what that was like. But no Henning, they aren't leprechauns.

I guess the moral of this particular story is avoid Manila like the plague. And the area of Tottenham!

Chapter 16 - Epilogue

No, this isn't the epilogue to the book, you dummy heads. If it was, it would be right at the end and not somewhere in the middle, wouldn't it? So just be patient with your ants in your pants and all will be revealed.

But since I mention middles, that's right where this next story takes place. In Alice Springs. Yes, despite the song, we all know where Alice is. Alice is right in the middle of Australia.

The 'Red Centre', as to which it's often referred. That would be because of the red sand in their deserts. Which is basically oxidation due to heavy amounts of iron in many of the rocks and them starting to rust.

If we are not laughing, we are learning.

After meeting a lovely chap by the name of Chris Cook, who was down in Adelaide doing spots, it was agreed that the following year, one must come up to Alice Springs to do a show with him and 'Red Centre Comedy'.

Chris happened to be living there with his wife and kids at the time working as a teacher. Well, a PE teacher, I believe, so not really a teacher at all. Just a facilitator of games in-between learning stuff. Not long before our splendid time together in the centre of Australia, we actually ended up doing some gigs together in The Netherlands. Enschede and Eindhoven to be more specific. And of course drinking together in Amsterdam. Where else? No weed though. One does not partake in such activity.

I'd never been to Amsterdam before, despite its party city reputation. Decriminalised weed and the red light district were never as appealing to me as other places around the globe. I shall leave all that to the potheads and the stag parties.

Still, another lovely chap by the name of Adam Fields arranged for me to be doing gigs in the aforementioned places, so over I went. I did actually end up in the red light district one evening, but that was completely by mistake. Honestly, guv!

I was following one of the canals to go and check out the Anne Frank museum, being the very cultured individual that I am interested in all things history, and I happened to stumble upon the red light district. I turned a corner and there it was! There, right before my very eyes, were all the women in the windows, waving at me and all of that business! 'Tis true that I did not intend visiting the red light district that day, but 'tis also true that I never made it to the Anne Frank museum.

I've got to be honest, Amsterdam was not at all the late night city I thought it was. Myself and Chris came back from the gig in Eindhoven and struggled to find a bar open later than 2am. We found a nice little Vietnamese-owned place not far from the red light district in the end though. That was nice. Very lovely and pleasant women serving us there.

It was also in Holland that Chris told me the story about how he was missing a middle finger. A horrible 'degloving' accident whilst working as a tour guide years ago in Australia. If you ever meet Mr Cook and want to hear the story, just make sure you're not eating anything at the time. Your food will go to waste.

Cut forward to Alice Springs and a lovely gig with a fun, if slightly challenging bunch of Northern Territorians in an intimate theatre venue. The highlight of which was me getting involved in an argument with a heckler about the Lion King 3. Long story, but he was talking about Die Hard 3 and I thought he was talking about the Lion King 3.

Basically, it was all about which movie Jeremy Irons was in. As I say, long story that I won't bore you with. I will say though that I did once win a $50 bet with a comedian in Melbourne who told me it was Alan Rickman who voiced Scar in the Lion King.

Of course it was the aforementioned Jeremy Irons. Money well and easily earned, I say. I know my Disney shit. Just ask the audience who were at that gig in Torremolinos.

Actually, no, don't!

Anyway, delightful show, and a trip to Uluru was absolutely magical. Rather than the overnight stay, I did the early morning start and late night return. It is a trip that is highly recommended. A truly amazing place to visit, it has to be said. Checking out the amazing monolith, the accompanying Aboriginal Dreamtime stories and finally eating dinner and drinking wine watching the sun setting over Australia's most famous landmark, which is truly an awesome and captivating sight. Do go if you can.

One night in Alice Springs however, Chris could not join me for drinks, so I went to a place called the Epilogue Lounge in the centre of town. It's a lovely and rather unassuming bar during the day, but the rooftop bar garden comes alive with '80s music some nights, which is always welcome by me.

Once Shalamar, The Jackson 5, The Fatback Band, The Real Thing and all those other banging tunes start blasting out, old snake hips Coppin has been known to throw a few shapes and bust a few moves on the dance floor.

Especially since I decided to hit the gin and tonics after a couple of beers that I was encouraged to drink by some of the people in the establishment who were at the show the night before and recognised me. One of which had the nickname 'Grasshopper', for reasons I can't remember now. I think maybe because he was small, with a rather large head and long limbs.

But I did get rather drunk that night, so my memory isn't necessarily the best.

He certainly wasn't a student of Kung Fu, I can tell you that much.

And I suppose it was the gin and tonics to blame for how the night ended. Which was basically me using my honourable Englishness to stand up for certain, shall we say, people of ethnicity, who have been downtrodden and disenfranchised in the past.

Let me explain.

Pretty much every night after I had hung out with Chris we went to the drive-thru McDonald's for late, drunk food. Like I said, I'm a cultured individual. But come on, let's face it, we really know McDonald's is very tasty indeed.

Did I mention that Neasden, my birth town, was the first location to have a drive thru McDonald's in the UK? Yep, true story. The model Twiggy was born there too. It's unlikely I'll ever be as famous as her, but you never know.

So, peckish as I was, I figured I would get another late McDonald's. But alas, a potential problem. At that time of night, about 1:30am, the restaurant was only drive thru and I was on foot. However, given I was a little bit, shall we say, on the lashed-up side, I thought I would give it a go trying to order through the intercom where cars pull up. Obviously, they were having none of it, so I thought I would try my luck at the window.

Again, no joy. Even though I was trying to have a laugh with them, it quickly dawned on me that as funny as I thought I was being, they just saw me as a drunken twat. To be honest, the Kiwi bloke serving at the window on the 'front line' seemed to find me rather amusing… trying to be a human car, but the chubby Australian flipping burgers behind him was much less impressed and giving me the beady evils. As such, I decided to wish them a good night, then move on and get something at the service station up the road, as per the Kiwi bloke's recommendation.

Now, here is the part. As I was walking across the forecourt of the fast food eatery, I passed a white car parked up awaiting an order and I heard someone shout something and some liquid hit the ground just behind my feet. Turned out it was some Northern Territory Aussie twat spitting some drink at me.

That was slightly sobering, I have to admit.

It didn't take long for me to work out that as a person of colour, they clearly thought - as some people have in the past - that I was either Indian or Aboriginal. In Alice Springs, probably Aboriginal, and had no doubt shouted something racially derogatory.

Now, I'm not one to kick off due to what is essentially some bloke just being a twat. But you know what? Some skinny young Australian bloke being a twat to somebody who he obviously believes is of an ethnic background so feels he can look down upon and abuse, is not on. Not on at all.

So I turned back and approached the car.

I think as soon as I opened my mouth and he heard my English accent, he realised he'd made a big mistake. I wasn't some disenfranchised Aboriginal lacking the confidence to stand-up to da white man, but rather a Brit not afraid to deal with this abusive nonsense. We own their country after all. And of course, I properly went full Winstone!

By that, I mean the well-known London ruffian actor, Ray Winstone. Not Dotty Winstone. In fact, I don't even know who Dotty Winstone is, but if there was some adorable old granny, the like of which was sweet and lovely to everybody and had a woolly cover on her teapot and had the surname Winstone, I'm guessing her name would be something like Dotty.

Basically, I wanted to give these little racist fuckers the impression I was somebody not to be trifled with. So, full Winstone, here we go. "Is there somefin' you wanna say to me, mate?" I followed up, "Did you just spit something at me?" as he continued his shocked look.

It appeared to be the bloke sat in the back of the car, so I directed my Winstone-ness at him.

"No!" he eventually and predictably replied, looking every bit like the sheepish, cowardly twat that he was.

"Well, one of you did!" Nik Winstone went back at him, "So, if you wanna give it some and 'ave a go, why don't you get out the car?"

"It wasn't me!" he continued with his denials.

So, turning my attention slightly to the front seat, I said to the one sat there, "So it was you then?"

"No, it wasn't me!" was the expected response I got from that question. Again, almost shrinking into his seat.

"Well, it was one of you, wasn't it?"

They both continued to look very sheepish and shake their spotty little heads.

It then occurred to me that I couldn't see the driver, so I bent down and leaned forward a bit to see who was in the driver's seat. Thinking it would probably be another one of their racist Aussie mates, I was surprised to see a woman of a similar age.

"You with these guys, are you?" I say to her. She clearly didn't want to be involved, so back to the two twats.

"Ah, I see now, you both trying to give it the big one in front of your girlfriend. That it?"

At that point, I got a response that almost made me crack up laughing, but given the drama school training that I've never had, I knew I couldn't break character. The bloke in the front exclaimed back to me in his bogan accent, "Actually, she's not ma girlfriend, she's ma wife!"

Like that somehow alters the situation! Does that mean you are clearly not guilty of the crime I'm accusing you of? Because you put a ring on this woman's finger means you're not showing off to impress her, as opposed to pre-marriage?

So, desperately resisting breaking character and starting to laugh my head off at his ridiculous comeback, but I thought to myself, *No! Winstone must continue!*

I took a bit of a step back and ramped it up a bit. "Right then. Since neither of you is man enough to admit you did it and you clearly want to impress this woman who is driving you around, why don't you both get out the car?" I said.

"Come on, out you get. You wanna give it Billy Big Bollocks in front of the lady, come on, let's 'ave it!"

As I suspected, nuffink! They just sat there getting whiter and more sheepish with every Winstone-esque word.

Then the best bit. Their food must have arrived, because all of a sudden the car tyres started spinning and they whizzed off away from the McDonald's, and as they did, from a more than safe distance away, one of the blokes leaned out of the car window and shouted back like the Aussie bogan that he was, "Real men don't fight!"

Then I really could allow myself to have a right old laugh. No, of course real men don't fight. What they actually do is spit at and abuse people they incorrectly consider to be lesser human beings than they are. Possibly in the vain hope that they impress some young woman. The sad thing is, maybe some young women might be impressed.

Although I doubt on this occasion, the particular woman driving the car thought much of the cowards sat beside her and behind her that night.

Either way, that was a very Alice Springs night indeed.

And I even managed to get some pretty decent food from the service station to take back to me hotel.

Actually, that's a lie. It was horrendously shit really.

Chapter 17 - The Huntsman Versus

At the start of 2015, it occurred to me that I have been paying for too much money in rent and bills back in the UK whilst I was away in Australia for three months of the year. As such I decided to give my flat up in San Lutonio and maybe sort out another place when I got back.

'San Lutonio' being Luton to those of you that don't know and understand the true nature of this idyllic Bedfordshire paradise that lies just north of London.

But then I decided, why not just stay in Australia throughout the summer (their winter. Topsy-turvy country) with friends and come back for the Edinburgh Fringe in August?

I would spend time throughout those chilly southern Australia winter months (and yes, it can be chilly down there in the winter, contrary to popular belief throughout the UK) visiting my uncle Terry and his family in Sydney, staying my friend Tina and her sister Cara in Melbourne, our Australian accountant Kerryn and her cute little boys Max and Ben, and last but not least, crazy Noel in Tasmania.

And yes, Noel is crazy. Certainly one of the more 'interesting' characters I've met and befriended throughout my jaunts to the Antipodes. He's a short, portly man, and he and his other half Mel are pretty loaded so he's very generous in his buying of beers and cooking of steaks, so he's alright by me.
Actually, I do like the mad bastard, despite him being a bit unhinged.

The only thing as odd as Noel are his trainers.

He's a bit too forward with details about him and his wife's sex life mind, but each to their own, I suppose.

Noel also seems to delight in sending me the occasional photo of his tiny penis with a ring through the tip and dumps he'd taken in the toilet. Yes, photos of shits he's done. I'm not sure which was more disturbing to be perfectly honest. Still, the occasional naked photo and video of his wife came through as well, which more than made up for the other unsavoury snaps.

All approved by her, of course. Consent is fundamental. Thanks again, James Nokise. He really is a good boy, James.

As well as being a mad fucker, he was a chef of sorts, so Noel had done quite a bit of time sorting out the cooking facilities in a few establishments around Australia, spending time away from his wife and kids, but then got headhunted to go and run the Diamond Island resort in Bicheno, on the east coast of Tasmania.

An absolutely beautiful part of the world, it has to be said. One of the most beautiful I have ever seen in fact.

Which reminds me actually, there was one time prior to Tassie that Noel was working at a place in the outback miles away from the family and feeling a bit, shall we say, 'lonely'. So he messaged me to ask if I still had the photos and videos of his missus and if so, could I send them to him as he didn't have them on him and neither did his wife back in Melbourne.

Sure mate, here you go. A selection of nudey photos and videos of YOUR WIFE!

Noel said I could stay at the resort he was running as long as I wanted, especially if I help him out around the place, and I think I managed three weeks in the end. Three weeks of amazing scenery and Noel treating me to beer, wine and some of the most amazing seafood I've ever eaten. Plenty of steaks and pies as well. Who ate all the pies..... and steaks.... and seafood? Me, that's who!

Drank the place dry of wine as well, I did. So proud of myself.

Then as darkness fell over Bicheno, they would have penguins come inland for the night and make their around the place as well. Such a waddling little treat.

Occasionally though, Noel would get drunk and think it was funny to throw kitchen knives and meat cleavers in your general direction, but you know, swings and roundabouts.

But then a couple of weeks in, it happened. The huntsman incident! A huntsman being a rather large species of spider found all over Australia.

As you know by now, I'm not exactly a fan of the eight-legged beasties. Many a person has also queried however, as to why I love the friendly neighbourhood wall-crawler so much, yet dislike spiders.

Well, a show at the Melbourne comedy festival some years back during which both spiders themselves and Peter Parker's alter-ego were mentioned numerous times, I was approached by an Israeli woman there with her fiancé, who told me she was a psychologist and that actually, a love of the web-slinging super-hero and dislike of spiders themselves might actually and rather bizarrely, make perfect sense.

She explained to me that as we all know, spiders are one of the world's biggest phobias and Spider-Man is one of, if not the most, popular of all superheroes.

Of course he is the best, that is not even a debate. And as previously discussed, he would easily beat up Wolverine. Any day of the week and twice on Sunday. Before and after roast beef, Yorkshire puddings, parsnips and gravy.

Apparently, she went on, one of the ways that psychologists treat phobias is to get people to face up to their fears and to try to see whatever it is they are afraid of in a positive light.

Therefore, children who have for whatever reason developed an irrational fear of spiders also subconsciously love Spider-Man because he's a hero who does good things. He's colourful, he has amazing powers, he saves lives and is also funny (unlike that miserable psychotic bastard Batman), so people and especially younglings dislike arachnids, yet adore and idolise the amazing Spider-Man. Interesting stuff.

Mind you, in all the years I'd been going to Australia, I had never encountered a spider. I'd not been surprised by one anyway. Certainly nothing like a potentially lethal redback or funnel-web and certainly not - despite countless Aussies trying to put the shits up me - one of these apparently very common and sizeable huntsmans.

Something I've always been curious about however, is the use of the word 'phobia' itself, certainly in more contemporary parlance. Like in words such as 'Islamaphobia' or 'homophobia'. Whilst we know it's ignorant and wrong to hate or dislike someone based on their religious beliefs or sexuality, I don't understand why it's considered a 'phobia'.

Like, racism and sexism are also wrong, but they are 'isms', not 'phobias'. I'm no psychologist (obviously) but surely the ignorant disdain for Muslims and gays would be more akin to not liking black people and members of the opposite sex, than spiders, right?

Like, if a spider suddenly appears out of nowhere, I tend to stiffen at the very sight of it. If I stiffen at the sight of a gay man, that's quite the opposite of a fearful feeling! Not the same at all really. Fearful of my newly realised passions, I suppose, but still, not a phobia.

Admittedly, if I saw a gay man crawling up my living room wall, I might be quite terrified! For starters where am I going to find a glass and a card that big?!

But on the other hand, I suppose a gay man the size of a spider, like say, a tarantula could be quite cute and I might just keep him around. Watch Netflix together and stuff. Cute. Anyway, I digress again.

So, one afternoon Noel decided to drag me to the pub just up the road for a bevvy. That turned into a few bevvies. And then a couple more. The plan was to get totally larruped, then crash out for a bit and then have more delicious food and booze at what I referred to as 'mission control'. Mission control being the main public area at the resort just up from the rooms, complete with bar, eating area and pool.

When I got back to my room, the now infamous (to me) number 22, I was proper lashed up and in need of a jimmy riddle, so I makes me way into the toilet.

As I'm standing over said toilet, I look up at a painting on the wall right in front of my very eyes. And as I do, I see what looks like a couple of pieces of string to the side of the painting. Now, even in my inebriated state I quickly calculate in me noggin that those strings are in the wrong place to hang a painting on a wall. I then notice that the strings are moving and subsequently disappear behind the painting itself!

I thought to myself, "That's got to be a spider! And judging by the size of those 'strings', a rather large one! Gotta be a huntsman!"

With retrospect, and it must've been the grog working its magic on the grey matter, I was surprisingly calm. A sober spider-fearing me might have panicked a bit more than drunken me did. If I had been less under the influence there's a good chance I would've set the whole of the resort ablaze. You know, just to be sure.

Right, I thought, got to have a proper look behind there to make sure my eyes and mind aren't playing tricks on me. But I don't want to get too close. In the absence of anything long and stick-like, I picked up an air freshener can and with an out-stretched arm, move the painting from being slightly against the wall and used the torchlight app on my phone to peer behind. And there I could see it. Illuminated eyes staring back in my direction. I moved back having heard tell that these things can jump. And I've seen them in action too. In the movie 'Arachno-phobia' and in the first Sam Raimi Spider-Man film.

The spiders running around town in the former of those two movies were actually huntsman spiders I discovered. Or 'Avon-dale' spiders to be more precise. After a number of 'auditions', studio bosses decided that this species could do all that was required for the specific movie scenes, so they asked the relevant Australian authorities if they could capture and take a load of them back to Hollywood to make them stars.

The authorities said it would be bad for the spiders and environment, so refused.

However, the producers discovered that huntsman spiders also lived in the Avondale area of Auckland, New Zealand. Apparently, they had snuck over there on perhaps railway sleepers years ago and due to the surrounding area not being conducive to their way of life, they just stayed in the area of Avondale.

It seems the New Zealand authorities were a lot more cool than the Aussies about the borrowing of the species. I'm assuming on the premise that they return them unharmed.

The Kiwis aren't monsters, after all. Well, except when they are playing rugby.

So, what to do about the immediate giant spider problem? My next sudden move surprised me yet again. It was decided between me and my drunken self that under absolutely no circumstances could this large hairy thing be allowed to escape into the bedroom and disappear under the bed or a chest of draws or something, otherwise I'd never get to sleep. So I closed the door, given the narrow spaces I know these Huntsmen can squeeze through, and put a towel along the bottom edge.

Thereby trapping both me and the huntsman in the room together! One of us is leaving this place in a container or glass and it ain't gonna be me, I thought. Hunt the Huntsman!

But what can I use to a) flush it out, and b) trap it?

Then I saw right before me both answers. A glass was by the sink for trapping and lo and behold, something I never thought

I'd ever need in a hotel room given my smooth dome...
a hairdryer! The wind and heat produced by that thing would
surely flush the fucker out from behind the artwork hanging on
the bathroom wall.

And it worked!

A few seconds of warm air in it's direction and the eight-
legged creature had to make its way round to the front of the
painting, where it just sat there. No doubt plotting in its tiny
spidery brain to jump at me and possibly munch on my head.
But boxing clever, I kept my distance.

Then I lunged! Trapping the beast under the glass, but also
being careful not to savage its outstretched pegs. I'm not an
animal after all. I wish this thing no harm.

Then it hit me that whilst I had the glass in hand and over the
huntsman, I had no card! For fuck's sake Coppin, glass AND

card! That's the combo for spider trapping and removal! All spider-hunters know this! A glass without a card is like an anvil without a hammer. Sonny without Cher. Batman without a young boy in green tights in his man cave for sexual gratification.

But alas! Within reaching distance was one of those tourist pamphlets about things to do in Tasmania. Not too much content, obviously, but enough to do the job. And it did! Huntsman trapped!

So, after a few iPhone photographs of said monster spider for social media, it was soon time to release it back into the wild. Obviously, a tricky situation. One does not want said monster

crawling up one's arm in the event of an awkward release gone wrong. Foolish Aussies say that huntsman spiders are harmless. Actually, the bite of such a beast can have a similar effect to that of a bee sting, and can cause serious uncomfortableness and even nausea. Whilst not actually deadly, not pleasant and certainly not 'harmless' either. Idiots.

You will be pleased to know that the release went smoothly downstairs in the bushes from room 22. Then I went back upstairs, into bed, and slept like a baby in a spider-free environment, before heading up to mission control later that night for more delicious grub, grog and if I'm lucky, another blade-throwing display from the madman.

Now if you are thinking that was the end of the spidery shenanigans, you are mistaken. It certainly was not! Two days later, just before settling down for the evening to watch some movies that Noel had downloaded onto a USB stick for me, I noticed another huntsman just above the curtains, curled up into a ball like it was trying not to be seen. But I have an eye for an arachnid! I can sense a spider!

Given that I've never had an encounter of any sort with a huntsman like this in about 10 years of visiting Australia, lightning surely can't strike twice in the space of a couple of days, so it had to be the same one! Cheeky bastard had made its way back inside! Probably seeking revenge for losing round one!

This time I managed to get the monster into a Tupperware container and leave it on the side for an hour or 2 to teach it a lesson. I poked holes in the top of the Tupperware container so it could breathe. I'm not a sadist.

Only this time I didn't make the same mistake releasing it anywhere near my room. I took my Tupperware with its scary dangerous cargo right down to the bottom of the resort and released it far away from room 22.

What happened to the huntsman from there, who knows?

Maybe the penguins ate it? Maybe it ate the penguins? Do penguins eat spiders? Do spiders eat penguins? From my research of both animals in the past, I don't think so, but there is a first time for everything.

Like encountering a giant spider whilst taking a piss.

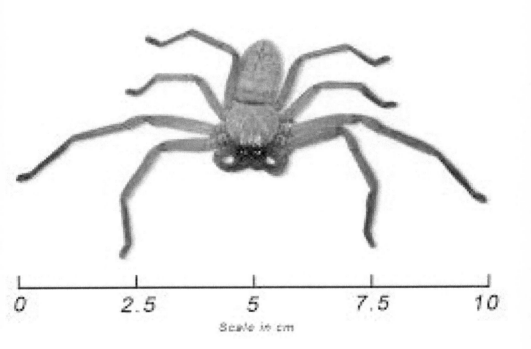

0	2.5	5	7.5	10

Scale in cm

Actual size

Chapter 18 - Harry!

Ten years, no spider attacks. Then that huntsman monster. Twice in the space of a couple of days! And does it stop there? No, of course it doesn't. For the last couple of years during the Adelaide Fringe, I have had the good fortune to stay in a lovely house owned by one of the most hard-working, selfless and charitable people I have ever met. Claire Victory. Yes, that is her real name.

Although given how successful she seems to be as a lawyer in South Australia, as well as life in general, maybe there is something to be said for names having an affect on your real life?

Nominative determinism I believe that is called. A friend of a friend put me in touch with Claire and she offered me free accommodation in her house in Oaklands Park. Top top person, I say. Basically because she knows how expensive it is to put on shows and likes to help per-formers out. So lovely. So, I spent a month living with her and her then housemate Shaun, who I am pleased to report is finally performing as his drag queen alter-ego, 'Judy Free'. Quite hot on Instagram she is.

Love a drag queen. I mean, who doesn't right? Not sure what to make of RuPaul's Drag Race however, which

Shaun got me to watch one day though. I didn't know what was going on. But maybe Nikita Copoff will be on there one day!

Don't ask, but one day she might appear at a Fringe somewhere with her 'Shag Queens'. Anyway, Claire has a garage which was very handy indeed for storing me bicycle for the month of the Fringe. Yes, hard as it is to believe, I own a bike in Adelaide and enjoy riding around in the sunshine to the beach, shops etc.

I happen to lose a good few pounds in Adelaide with all the cycling and swimming activity, but then always put it back on in Melbourne where the weather isn't quite as good at that time of the year during the Comedy festival, I don't have a bike and spend far too much time in the 24-hour Greek food restaurant, Stalactites. An institution it is! Lots of great Chinese and other fooderies in that fine city too. Not good for the waistline, I can assure you.

Wait, did I mention Stalactites in a previous chapter? I think I did. Alright, take it easy. Blimey!

One day about a week into the Fringe in Adelaide, I went into the garage to do some very minor maintenance on the bike, which was no more than adjusting the saddle I believe, and as I reach down into a toolbox looking for a spanner or some such tool, a huge redback spider comes up and around on it's web which spanned the toolbox and a load of other boxes.

Obviously, I jumped back and in my mind was like, "Holy shit-sticks!". Which I am sure came out of my mouth in the form of a squeal. Redbacks aren't anywhere near as sizeable as huntsman spiders, but as I'm sure you know, are among the world's most venomous spiders. And as redbacks go, this one was no small thing. As much as I am no fan of arachnids, I still tended to the bike keeping the thing well in my sights the whole time.

The next day, I told Claire and Shaun about this deadly spider appearing in their garage. Thinking that they would need to know so as not to be surprised like I was or worse, possibly succumb to its killer venom in an unexpected and unsolicited onslaught. They both replied, "Oh, you've met Harry! He's our pet redback, We haven't seen him for a while" Like, er.....WHAT?!?! 'Pet' and 'redback' are not two words to be used back-to-back in the same sentence in my opinion.

Some people need to recognise potential dangers, man. Is not being fearful of spiders an Aussie thing? I don't think so, because when I was researching spiders ahead of my first trip to Australia (yes, I did that), I learned that arachnophobia is most prevalent in westernised countries like the UK, USA and Australia. Yep, the Aussies are scared of spiders just like us, despite what they try to say when putting down us 'softcock' POMs.

Although another thing I learned about through course of me spidery research and readings was a rather astonishing story from Grafton maximum security prison in New South Wales. As the story goes, prison officers found a load of hypodermic needles in a jail cell and suspected they were being utilised for serious drug use.

They weren't wrong, but it wasn't the kind of drugs that they would normally expect. All was revealed when officers also found a load of redback spiders in a jar that the prisoners were breeding, like pets! Breeding and making pets of some of the world's most potentially deadly spiders! And that's not all. It turned out that they were 'milking' the spiders for their venom, watering it down and injecting it for a high!

I know, right? Crazy times! As somebody who really doesn't like spiders - or drug use for that matter, I found this whole business very unsavoury indeed. But also hugely impressed! I mean not just to think of doing such a thing, but also calculating the correct dosage to get the right buzz without killing or doing serious harm to oneself.

I mean, thinking about it, in a historical reversal, can
Australia please send their criminals over here?!
These guys would make brilliant scientists and doctors!

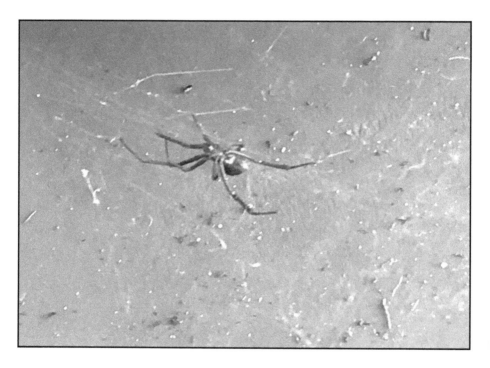

Harry, the pet redback spider!

Chapter 19 - Wanderer

One night after a gig in West London, a fellow performer decided he wanted to go and have a drink in a strip club. Not really my thing (honestly, guv), but some comedians are sleazy like that. And his mate was the DJ in the establishment and it was one of very few places open for a late beverage, so in we went.

So whilst he was off leering at the ladies and conversing with his mate on the decks, I was at the bar treating meself to half a pint of liquid gold when I was approached by a young pretty woman in I'd say her late 20s. God knows why it wasn't a full pint, maybe I was having an off day. I offered her a drink and she politely refused, preferring just to chat rather than have an alcoholic beverage.

She asked what I did and why I was there, so I gave her the rundown as to how I came to be in said venue. She seemed very nice indeed actually, so I in turn enquired about where she was from, noticing that she had a Latino look. "I am from Brazil," she told me.

Not quite sure how to respond to that, the first thing that came out of my mouth was, "I've always loved the Brazil football team. "Are you any good at football?" immediately internally chastising myself for my ridiculous opening gambit!

To my surprise, she replied, "Yes! I was the best football player at my school."

Again, not quite being sure where to go from there, I went on "Did you know that in Brazil you have the world's largest spider? The Goliath bird-eating spider! It can grow to the size of a dinner plate!"

She looked at me quizzically and said, "No, I didn't know that."

Taking her demeanour to mean she clearly wanted to know more, I went on. "Brazil is also home to the world's most venomous spider, the Brazilian wandering spider!"

Again, a quizzical look that I took for further interest in my vast knowledge of South American arachnids. So, having her full attention, I proceeded!

"However, the Brazilian wandering spider - also known as the banana spider on account of the fact that it has been seen in many shipments of bananas from your country - whilst being the most venomous spider, is not considered the most dangerous." More looks of interest.

"The title of most dangerous spider goes to the male Sydney funnel-web spider in Australia. I know," I went on. "How can one be the most venomous at the other be the most dangerous? Well, let me explain. Whilst it's proven through thorough experimentation that the Brazilian wandering spider's venom could kill more animals based on the same amount being injected as other spiders, it doesn't always deliver a full envenomation. And maybe not even any venom at all. More of a warning bite. So if bitten by a Brazilian wandering spider, you might get a full dose of its potentially lethal venom, in which case you could die, a little dose which might make you a little bit sick, or just a couple of pinpricks. Whereas the pugnacious, vicious bastard that is the Sydney funnel-web spider, will give you a full envenomation every time it strikes! So you see, one is more venomous but the other is actually more dangerous."

At that point, she turned and walked off and started speaking to somebody else. As they say, a little knowledge is a dangerous thing.

As is an overactive mouth, it seems.

But still not as dangerous as a Brazilian wandering or funnel web spider though.

Mum, Danny and me!

Chapter 20 - Mum

Now, if you bothered to read the dedication, you will know it was made to my dearly beloved mummy and daddy. Or as I like to call them, mum and dad. I'm not some poncey upper-middle-class twat after all.

Of course, I will completely understand if you skipped past those book formalities because you were so keen to get stuck in to my global stories of international hilarity.

It seemed only right to dedicate it to the two people whom without which none of this would be possible. And I'm not talking about the fact that me old man put his little swimmers into me old dears eggs producing the bundle of joy that was me.

And FYI, I was indeed a bundle of joy to carry around for a few months too. No pregnancy problems at all. That might be mainly because apparently when my mum was pregnant with my older brother Danny, she had chronic toothache throughout all of her mouth. So when she learned she was pregnant with me, she had all her teeth removed and dentures put in because the pain was so bad previously.

Yeah bro, that's what you did to mum. You squirming around in her belly was literally pulling teeth.

I've often thought that she was winding us up with that, but it's apparently true.

As my brother and my dad will know all too well, that's me mum. From as young as I can remember she had issues with a bad back, ulcers, migraines and eventually hip replacements.

Never the most healthy of people, but she never gave up. Just got on with shit, man. A right old trouper was dear old Chrystal Leslie Coppin. She could never do enough for us and pretty much everybody she knew. And all done with a smile on her face.

A proper Norf London working class woman from a working class family. Two sisters and six brothers. No TV back then, I guess. No Netflix and chill. Just shagging and babies. Although rather amusingly I did find out recently from a chat with the youngest of all the brothers, uncle Max, that the reason grandma Violet got with granddad Joe, was because the guy she was seeing before him wanted a big family and she didn't. Joe told her that he wasn't interested in a big family, so she hooked up with him. Lying, dirty, randy old git. Knocked up Violet time and time again and then went off to war.

Another right old trooper it seems. In the bedroom as well as on the battlefield!

A big norf of the river Thames family and all Arsenal fans. That red and white also runs through my veins to this day. Although the last couple of years post-Arséne Wenger have been a bit of a rough ride.

Of course in the end he had to go, I guess. I did love the Wenger, but something was missing towards the end of his reign. But then, it is a sad indictment on modern day and Premier League football that three FA Cups in four years is not seen as a sufficient success.

Still, it wasn't that all-important 'top four trophy'. Bit of a silly thing for Arséne to say that, but elements of truth to it nonetheless, given the amount of money to be had in qualifying for the UEFA Champions League.

(Editor's note - how the Hell did you manage to turn a tribute chapter about your mum into a random rant about Arsenal!)

As well as looking after myself and my brother most of the time, my mum also made extra money looking after other people's children. She was funny too, the old dear. A right old laugh, Chrystal. One of the funniest stories she told us was the time where my dad was using the bathroom and she really needed to go to the toilet.

Myself and my brother grew up in a small one bedroom maisonette in Neasden, Northwest London. Yes, all four of us in there until meself and Danny moved out. Right cosy it was.

Anyway, it seems Chrystal was desperately in need of a download, but my dad being the old West Indian scamp that he was, not realising the severity of the situation, refused to come out. Probably busy plucking the whiskers out of his face. He used to do that. I do remember him using an electric shaver as a small kid, but later in life, I would often see him looking in the mirror pulling his stubble out with tweezers. Not only highly unusual, but must've been painful. Must have leather for skin.

So, there was Chrystal desperate for a number two and my dad being silly and holding his ground.

My brother, Danny Long-Legs seems to be taking up most of this photo with his pegs, whilst I appear to be asphyxiating my mother!

So, me poor old mum, with nobody else being in the flat at the time, had to drop her payload in the bin in the kitchen!

I must admit, I thought she was tugging my chain when she dumped that story on me, but apparently it's true. And of course being the dutiful, discrete son that I am, I told an audience of about 150 people at a charity gig that she came to in East London. I think the audience - consisting of my girlfriend at the time Tina, all of her family, many friends and work colleagues and even auntie Rita and uncle Leslie - thought it was both hilarious and shocking at the same time. I think they were also quite embarrassed for my mum but good old Chrystal laughed along.

That's Chrystal, a good old British sense of humour and always very supportive of myself and my brother. I remember years ago, she said of a birthday card I bought for her about the printed message inside, "I'm sure you didn't read what it said, but it's probably one of the nicest things I've read in a card." What the card said was, "Thank you mum, for letting me be myself."

She was correct. I, of course, wrote kind lovely birthday words in the card but I rarely read the text inside. Maybe I picked that card subconsciously because every word rang true?

Her continued support, would of course be much appreciated to this day.

However, back in 2004, I was on my way back from a gig in Maidstone at a pub called the Walnut tree. A pub that has been running comedy for about 30 years now, and seen many a now superstar grace it's unusual and often tricky to play, L-shaped room.

I was on the train back and thought of getting off the night bus from central London in Neasden - which was en route to where I was staying in Preston Road, near Wembley at the time, to maybe crash at my parents place. It was a small space, but it would've saved me a lot of time bearing in mind I was on a very early shift at King's Cross Station the next morning.
That and it had been a little while since I'd seen the old dear and the old man.

It wasn't just that - and I'm no spiritual person by any stretch - but something in the back of my mind and maybe in my stomach made me feel I should pop by, but then I thought no, I wouldn't get there until at least 2am, so rather than disturb their sleep, I continued the extra few miles back to my flat.

I remember waking up at just before 5:30am, to a text from my brother not long before my alarm was due to go off to get up for my early shift. He said that mum had been taken to Central Middlesex hospital, after dad had come back from a night shift and discovered her unconscious in bed because she'd had a possible stroke. As I said before, mum was never the most healthy of people throughout her life, so given the fact that she would often visit the hospital, I asked him how bad it was. Should I rush down there now, or should I go after or leave early from work? I had taken way too much time off work as it was in recent weeks.

He said he didn't know, but he was going to join dad, so I jumped out of bed, got dressed and made my way down.

That was a long day, I can tell you. My mum had had a massive brain haemorrhage and was hooked up one of those horrendous machines, but the trouper she was, she was fighting on. Sadly, in the end, it was in vain. The bleed was simply too severe. Even when we all had to make that decision to turn off the life support machine - my dad, my brother and myself - she hung on for a good while.

Sadly, Chrystal Leslie Coppin passed away at the age of 64. I wish she could've come to more shows, other than just the couple she made when I was a fledgling comedian. I would like to think she would've been proud of my globetrotting comedic exploits.

But I guess, as heartbreaking as these things can be, death is sadly a part of life. And if you believe in an afterlife or spirituality in any way, shape or form, then I suppose dear old Chrystal is up there watching every show I do, all over the planet.

Blimey mum, you must be pretty bored by now.

xxx

Chapter 21 - Dad

The old man, yep, he is still with us.

Stafton Ishmael Coppin AKA 'Sandy'. That's what my mum used to call him, as did friends and his work colleagues.

A friend of mine years ago, upon learning my dad's real Christian name, said it sounded like a racehorse. I suppose you could imagine that being the name of a horse running in the 3:15 at Cheltenham.

His brothers had equally colourful names; Myron, Sylvain and Darnley. Colourful names and interesting characters, but that seems to be quite a West Indian thing.

And my West Indian family are certainly quite amusing it has to be said. Stories for another time maybe.

But yes, my dad is from the Caribbean island of Barbados. I often think about how tough things must have been for him - as well as many other immigrants - all those years ago, but he never really spoke about it. Like my mum, but in rather different ways, he just got on with things. Another reason why today's snowflakes tend to get up my sniffer. My mum and dad had it tough, but they never carried any of those proverbial chips round on their shoulders and they never moaned and whinged about anything. And certainly didn't blame anyone or the world around them for any difficulties.

I like to think they passed some of that on to me. Must admit I do like to whinge about certain things though.

Whilst my mum could often be no-nonsense, she didn't
brandish nunchucks. Nor did she walk down the street
waving a string of sausages around. That would be silly. It's
just that when I did this caricature many moons ago, she had a
collapsible walking stick. Well, that's what it's meant to be.

In case you were wondering, no, my dad never played for the mighty West Indies cricket team. But if you ever go to Barbados, try the flying fish. Very tasty indeed. And watching them actually fly is a sight to be hold. From the sea, to the air, to your plate.

When my mum passed away, I moved back in with my dad for a while. And at one point he did question why I had left my secure job on London Underground Limited for this itinerant minstrel existence of uncertainty. I've always maintained however, that there is actually a lot more certainty with regard to self-employment and stand-up comedy than some might think. In that you are a lot more in control of your own destiny. Things can be hard, and in ways people might not think, but nobody can really sack you as such... except maybe a pandemic!

You can't tell your 'audience' on London Underground to "fuck off" and not just get away with it, but get laughs and sometimes booked for more work.

My dad shows what he thinks of me posing (with long hair and no beer belly!) in Barbados in the early 90s.

So, it's completely understandable how an old West Indian father would find that difficult to wrap his head around, however. But what my father doesn't understand, probably because I don't explain it fully to him, is that I do actually have pensions and savings schemes on the go, as well as the London Underground Limited pension squirrelled away after nearly 15 years on the job. If he reads nothing else in this book, I will make sure he read this paragraph!

My dad was generous enough to pass on some of his savings to myself and my brother a few years ago too, some of which did go towards paying off debts accrued from travelling the world and stumping up for festivals and shows that didn't quite always turn a profit, but do now thanks in many ways, to my dad. Also, much was invested. A lot of my brother's dosh was spent on his house in Luton and kids, so it's understandable that me old man might consider me to be less responsible. I don't have such assets and harassments in my life, rather choosing thus far to live a more nomadic stress and care-free lifestyle.

And more ironic I suppose, is that my dad left Barbados at the age of 18 to come all the way over to the UK in search of a new life. I don't think I've done anything quite as brave or risky as that in my entire life! Yes, he saved up all his pennies from working in a sugar factory and jumped on a British West Indian Airways flight for 75 quid. Sounds like a right ol' bargain that, but I'm sure it wasn't cheap back in those days. How he arranged accommodation and work all those years and miles ago has me scratching me noggin when I think about it.

I mean, there wasn't any Internet or anything! Spoken like a true millennial, I know, but I'm way too old to be one of those. I must ask him how me managed that someday. Either way, I'm confused and proud in equal measure.

My dad has always been way more supportive of myself and my brother than I think we've sometimes given him credit for. Watching shows though? I think I can only remember him coming to one. And weirdly, it wasn't a stand-up comedy show.

When I worked on London Underground Limited, my good friend and manager at the time Andy Antony - also slightly responsible for me getting into comedy to be honest - roped me into a couple of charity shows that were bordering on drag acts. One in particular was this performance based around the movie *Grease!* More cheesey than a block of Wensleydale, but a great movie nonetheless. Let's not talk about the sequel. I've not seen it, but from what I have heard, I hope I never will.

The charity show was an all-singing, all-dancing display of a number of us LUL staff miming and prancing around the stage at the Met Club in Wembley Park. The Met Club being a London Transport owned sports club for the workers on the Metropolitan Line. We were dressed in all sorts of silly costumes, but there was a solo performance I did that I believe my dad still has on VHS video to this day.

Oh, that's right younglings, VHS video. Just imagine a big brick-shaped Blu-ray disc. A massive black one! Feel free to look up VHS versus Betamax. VHS was slick and good with symmetrical cassettes, Betamax was chunky top-loading shite with cassettes that looked like a one-eyed plastic monster.

Anyway, my solo performance was pretty much me in a leather jacket, jeans and wig, miming to a song from the soundtrack called rather ironically, 'Sandy'. Yep, me dressed as John Travolta's character, Danny Zuko, singing a song with a title being the same name as my dad, as he looked on.
Creepy or what?

But of course, I couldn't mime it to myself, could I? In the absence of anybody doing Olivia Newton-John's part for my solo section, I was basically traipsing around singing to a glove puppet raccoon, which about a third of the way into the song I pulled out from the inside pocket of my leather jacket.

And as if the leather jacket and wig weren't enough to give authenticity to my performance, the choreographers - for want of a better word - also got me to 'white-up'. Yes, I performed as Danny Zuko, miming the song to a toy raccoon with my dad's name, with white-face on!

And apparently everybody was fine with that. Strange, isn't it? A brown guy whiting up is okay, but a white person blacking up, not okay!

And I have had many a discussion about this. We know it is at least very much frowned upon when white man does black face, but I would counter that, if say, a white man is a fan of Marvel's Luke Cage AKA Power Man and wants to attend a fancy dress party as his hero, why can't he black up?

In fact, I had a conversation very recently with a few friends, and once again, the German Comedy Ambassador Mr Henning Wehn about this very thing.

The conversation centred around a scenario we joked about with regard to my girlfriend and I getting married in a mixture of Wizard of Oz (she's a huge fan) and Marvel superhero costumes. We decided that should this ever happen, Henning could come as a German character. The first one we thought of was the Red Skull. He could paint his face red and voila! Red Skull.

Actually, there is a villain called Armless Tiger Man, but no one had heard of him. And yes, that is a genuine Marvel character. A German bloke in a skin-tight yellow spandex outfit, with no arms and sharp teeth. He basically goes around kicking and biting people. Make mine Marvel!

But both super-villains. No heroes. Why are there no German superheroes? Actually, I think we all know the answer to that question.

However, I would obviously go as Spider-Man, so no face paint needed there.

But here's the thing… there were a couple of female friends at the table so we discussed who they might go as. She-Hulk and Gamora were the first two female superheroes mentioned and as such, a good dose of green paint on the face would be in order. Somebody then brought up Storm from X-Men. At that suggestion, everybody was of the opinion that the two white women at the table would not be able to black-up, since Storm AKA Ororo Munroe is of African origin.

Which presents the interesting question and debate. If you can red-up for the Red Skull, green-up for She-Hulk, why can one not put black or brown make up on to represent an African character?

I think I'll leave that one to the middle-class white guilt people to discuss. They seem to have all the answers for us darkies, after all.

Wait! Hold the phone! NIGHTCRAWLER! From the X-Men! He's from Bavaria, in Germany and one of the good guys! So, yes, Henning can be him and 'blue up'. And maybe even wear a tail. Kinky!

(Editor's note - Again, how the Hell did a chapter about your dad morph into another Superhero monologue?)

Chapter 22 - Tony

I suppose it would be wrong not to give Tony Hadlames a bit of a mention here with regards to comedy origins. Reason being, he kind of did give me a bit of a push to take up treading the boards as it were.

Or with regard to stand-up comedy - as opposed to acting - treading the sticky beer-stained carpet, since many gigs and certainly the earlier ones are in rooms above or below pubs.

I should also add that myself and an old flatmate 'Ollie' were kind of responsible for getting Tony and his wife Yvonne together. Tony being a work colleague of Ollie's and Yvonne being a long-term friend of mine. It took her some time to get there mind. She really wasn't a fan when I first met her, which was when I was seeing her bestie 'Claude'. Or Claudette to give her her full name.

But over time, 'Vonnie' came to realise what a thoroughly good egg I am.
Especially when she went through a break-up from a bit of a dodgy bloke and I was always around to go drinking with her. Of course I was. The bloke was a bit of a crazy Scot from what I remember too. Typical of those lot. Kidding guys! You know I think we're good together. *Och aye the noo* and all that Brave-heart business.

One night drinks were arranged in the Rat & Parrot pub in Harrow, so I brought out Yvonne and Ollie brought out Tony. The rest is 20 years of marital bliss (is that even possible?), and of course I was the Best Man at the wedding. The clue is in the title of the job, 'just' ushers. Great speech I did too, I might add. I was as nervous as all shit though. People thought it would be a walk in the park for me since I'd been doing stand-up comedy for a little while, but obviously the level of expectancy with regards to the funny obviously goes up, and of course, it is different in a big room when its not set up for comedy and when you know half the audience personally.

It was quite funny when the master of ceremonies and DJ tried to give me some advice about how to talk into a micro- phone and embarrassingly apologised later when he found out I did comedy. Yep, stick to spinning those decks mate. Or nowa- days, playing iTunes from your phone. I'm not saying it's a lot easier being a DJ, but well, it is.

The speech was simple in the end though. Pay a huge com- pliment to how lovely the bride looks, then rip the piss out of your friend. Especially when just a week previously, the dopey bastard had fallen over in two feet of water in a swimming pool nightclub in Spain and nearly drowned because he can't swim.

That and he was wearing a kilt, since his dad was Scottish. Fortunately for myself and the ushers, Yvonne put her foot down with regards to us wearing trousers. Thanks Yvonne. No skirts for us. Kidding guys! We're good together, right? Flower of Scotland and all that Robert the Bruce business.

It's also worth noting that another friend out that fateful night was Kirstie, a 6ft tall redheaded model who I used to hang out with because she lived in a flat near Baker Street station, where I worked in the ticket office at the time. I met her going through the station on a regular basis, as did her flatmate Cat Deeley. Yes, that Cat, from TV presenting fame. That Cat used to work in our favourite post-shift pub the Allsop Arms round the corner from the station, so served me many a pint back then.

In fact, one could say that the lovely Cat Deeley regularly pulled one off for me.

But away from the 'Carry On' movie humour, I also happened to be temporarily staying at their flat in Colindale when Tony and Yvonne's first born, Taron, was conceived and brought home from the hospital.

Obviously I didn't actually watch or take part in the conception, or hear Tony's probably 20 seconds of baby-making shagging through the walls, but it happened. Taron used to be such a good boy as a proper Spider-Man fan as well, but then his stupid dad Tony, turned him to the dark side and he became more of a Batman fan. Fool!

For my good friend Taron, Happy Birthday, Nik

"Turned to the dark side by his father!"

Still, after their daughter Georgia was born, Christian came along and he is a proper Spider-Man fan, so good lad there.

By the way, in case you haven't realised, Tony is the bloke with the gargantuan head from the horrible bar in the previous Torremolinos show story. Actually, and rather ironically now I think about it, that nightclub pool was in Torremolinos! That was where I'd arranged 6 nights away for his stag do. He was drowning in two feet of water and 20 years later, I'm drowning on stage in front of a load of miserable shitbag expats. What goes around comes around.

After years of deliberation it was big head Tony who gave me a bit of a shove to do stand-up comedy. I was out with Ollie and other transport budlings in the West End, and Kebba, the other chubster from the Spain story was in attendance and started up about something or other and I tore him a new arsehole with some good old-fashioned cussing. Gave him a right old doing over.

This was the first time Tony had ever met me I believe, and he was mightily impressed with how I completely ran roughshod over Kebba with a good tongue lashing, so he said to me, "You're really funny, have you ever thought about writing comedy?"

I told him I had thought about doing stand-up comedy for a little while now, so with that encouragement as opposed to most people not taking it seriously at all, it was that bit more encouragement I needed at the time which helped push me over the comedy edge. And the rest as they say, is history.

However, to my mind and unfortunate seeing eye, the funniest thing Tony ever did was one night back at the flat with him and 'Godzilla' Yvonne in Colindale before I was a spare room houseguest for about a year. We used to joke about her being Godzilla, because she would invariably go to bed before us and be banging on the wall because we dared to have a conversation in her absence and we would sit there imagining her big Godzilla head would burst through the wall to properly shout at us. I mean, we were obviously always considerate enough to keep our voices down to almost a whisper, but you know, she had to get up for work in the morning and all that. Selfish Godzilla woman!

We may have played a bit of Trivial Pursuit, or just been out on a lash up previously, I can't remember. I mean, I beat Tony so many times at Trivial Pursuit it's hard to even remember whether we played that night or not. TonyHadlames, a head the size of a small planet with a brain the size of a lentil.

Anyway, after a good few beers and wines as myself and Tony put the world to rights, as we often did back then, as well as rubbishing each other's football teams, I crashed out on their quite comfy sofa. He is a Chelsea supporting twat by the way, and probably the most annoying person to talk to about football. Yeah, that and he turned his eldest son Taron to the dark side of Twatman. The thing is, I don't think Tony is even a Batman fan, he just likes to be contrary and thinks he's cool by being all dark and twisted like that psycho Bruce Wayne.

So there I was crashed on the sofa. Must've been about 3:30am when my head hit the armrest and I took to Slumberland.

Next thing I knew, I'm waking up what must've been a couple of hours later at about 5:30am. I was still very tipsy with a groggy noggin, so I think I managed to open one crusty eye. And there, right in the corner of the room, was probably one of the most horrific sights I think I have ever seen. And that is even taking into account the Batman versus Superman movie.

Tony, absolutely sloshed out of his massive Pluto-sized napper, staggering around in the corner of the darkened room, drunkenly coughing in his chubby clenched hand singing Buddy Holly's Peggy Sue to himself. Through my one open eye, I looked at him for about a minute before going back to sleep and trying to get that disturbing image out of my head.

That image being a far from slim Tony wearing nothing but green underpants and one red sock. It was dark, so the colours might not have been correct, but just those items are what he was wearing. I have often questioned as to why he got himself so naked and removed just one sock and not the other one, but I've been too busy trying to get that picture out of my mind ever since. As the old saying goes, some things you just can't unsee. As well as world affairs and football, myself and Tony had often debated who was the greatest entertainer of all time, Elvis Presley or Michael Jackson. Putting certain dodgy practices, accusations and court cases aside, it's Wacko Jacko for me all the way.

However, myself and grumpy contrary Hadlames had agreed that were his life not cut so tragically short, it may have ended up being Mr Buddy Holly. We felt his songs at least we're pretty fantastic even if he wasn't quite the showman that Elvis and Jacko were. Of course, not when they are renditions performed by a large-headed pudgy bloke in a state of hideous undress fuelled by copious amounts of Jack Daniels.

Trust me when I tell you I had to reduce the size of his head for this caricature!

Chapter 23 - A Scary Story

Alright, so, up until this point I think we've had enough comedy stories. Or at least I hope we have. So, I reckon it's about time I told you a scary story.

Many of you out there will have acquired this book thinking it was comedy story after comedy story after comedy story. As such, you might want to skip this one especially if you are faint of heart.

But if you are still reading this section, then you are okay with a bit of scariness.

The scary story takes place on Cottesloe beach in Perth. That would be the bright, colourful, picturesque version in sunny Australia, not the drab, dreary, bleak version up the M90 from Edinburgh in rainy Scotland.

Now, despite hearing about some pretty dangerous things that lurk around these parts, myself and a number of comedian and producer friends were having a right old jolly splash around in the clear blue waters of Western Australia.

I had been to this beach before of course, many times in fact. The first time being many years previous with my mate Dave Holland. Dave is now plotted up in Perth, but I know him from when he used to run a pub called The Bull, in Shepperton, just south of London. Through a mutual friend, I ended up running a weekly Thursday night comedy show there.

In all honesty, it was quite a rough affair, but also a right old laugh. I made some good mates there. One of whom being

General Zod. Well, he went by the name of Zod, but being a superhero fan, I gave him the 'General' prefix because of the character featured in the movie Superman 2.

Zod was a serious looking man in his late 30's I would say, and he used to sit on a high table in the middle of the room at almost every show. He looked like he wanted to head-butt you as soon as look at you, but he was a jolly nice bloke really. A decent Arsenal fan as well who had a season ticket and used to follow them all over Europe, so he was always going to be alright by me.

According to Dave, Zod also had a friend called Philip Venus. Not overly unusual in itself, but apparently - and Dave swears by this - Philip named his son 'Manfrom'. Yep, I shit you not. I was like, 'No way", but both Dave and General Zod swear 'tis true. Dave is a Yorkshireman by birth, so even if you can't trust him for good reason, you can surely trust an Arsenal fan.

Let's just hope Philip's son never gets stopped by the police because he's going to have a right fun time telling them his name.

"Manfrom Venus? Really? Right, in the back of the car, son."

Anyway, because I knew the reputation of Cottesloe beach and promptly told him so on the way there, Dave, being the gruff Northern git that he is, said to me something along the lines of, "Don't be such soft southern bastard. More people are killed every year from bee stings in Australia than shark attacks!" That may be statistically true, but I was quick to point out that that number would certainly change if sharks could fly! I'm going in the water. That's where sharks live.

Which is why I've always been intrigued by the term 'shark infested waters'. No, sharks live in the water, surely when humans enter the ocean, the waters become 'human infested'?

But you can't argue with Dave. One time he came back from dinner with his (no doubt long-suffering) wife at about 9pm and lounging around right there in the middle of his living room was a highly venomous Australian snake. Obviously, Dave calls up the local snake catcher straight away requesting his presence to remove said lethal serpent.

In true Australian fashion, the bloke on the phone said, "No worries mate, I'll come round first thing in the morning," to which gruff no-nonsense northerner Dave replied, "No you fookin' won't, you'll come round right now, ya bastard!"

And he did. Snake, dealt with.

Anyway, the scary story!

So, we are having a jolly old time for about ten minutes in the sea, or ocean rather, and then about thirty yards out from us, a massive fin comes up out of the water! Seeing this we are obviously quite shocked. Especially when it starts moving in our direction.

We look back towards the beach and realise we've actually come out a surprising distance. There is no way we would get back to the shore in time, so we just have to watch this fin approaching, as it moves very quickly in our direction.

Obviously, we are shitting ourselves, but there is nothing we can do but just stand there and hope it doesn't notice us.

It starts to get closer and closer and closer, but then we realise, "Thank God, it's not a fin, it's a Norwegian!"

Ha! Suckers!

It wasn't a scary story at all. It was just a shit joke all along! Yep, one that I have told many times. Of course, I realise after writing it down for the first time, the fin/Finn bit doesn't quite work. But fuck off, it's a doozy of a shit joke verbally!

But I do now sense the disappointment of those that stuck with this particular story thinking it was going to be scary. But alas, don't be let down, because I do have a scary story for you. And it is one of comedy scariness.

Right after Perth Fringe World, the Adelaide Fringe takes place. This particular year I had decided I wanted to do a free entry midweek show where I just try out new material. At the end of every show I decided I would tell a shit joke just to see how the audience reacted. One Tuesday night it was the Finn/Norwegian joke's turn for an outing. Told pretty much as I've written it here. There were about 50 people in the small intimate space, most of whom groaned at my joke. And rightly so, because let's face it, it's shit.

However, there was a young Aussie couple sat right in the front row, Tyler and Kate. I can't really remember if her name was *Kate*, it may have been Louise or something, but for the purposes of simplicity, let's stick with *Kate*. But Tyler was definitely his name because you never forget a name that is also an occupation. Tyler is absolutely pissing himself at the joke. So I have to address this imbalance in the room. As such I question as to why Tyler is laughing so hard when everybody else is groaning.

"Fucking brilliant joke, mate", he replies in his friendly bogan Aussie accent.

"No mate, it's not. It's shit," I remind him.

Still, Tyler maintains that he loves the joke and comedy being subjective and all of that business, I accept his love of my joke.

Girlfriend Kate however, is just staring at me looking extremely perplexed indeed. So I asked her, "Are you ok there, Kate?"

"Yeah, I'm fine", she replies and again, in a very friendly bogan Aussie accent. Bogan love bogan, innit!

Not having this, I ask a different question. "You didn't get the joke, did you, Kate?" "No," she replies, rather honestly.

"Ok," I say, "Don't worry, I'll explain the joke to you. I'm like the Microsoft paperclip, I'm here to help." A reference that a woman in her early 20's now gets even less than the joke I just told her.

"Right. I know you are Australian and 10,000 miles away on the other side of the world, but in Europe there is a country called Finland. Did you know that, Kate?"

"No", she replies.

"Well, if we're not laughing, we're learning, Kate. So, people from the country of Finland in Northern Europe, we call Finnish. Or, Finns for short."

Kate continues to stare at me, confused. So I go on.

"So, it wasn't a Finn from Finland, it was a Norwegian from Norway."

Still looking confused, Kate says, "Why Norway?"

Now I'm confused. As are the 50 or so other people in the room. I mean, how can you not get that? But you know, bogans and all that. So I go on.

"Well Kate, Norway, like Finland, is also a country in Northern Europe and they are quite close together, so I mistook a Finnish person for a Norwegian person."

Still confused, Kate asks, "Why a Norwegian?"

At this point I think Kate is getting more laughs than anything I've said throughout the entire 60 minute show!

"Because Kate, they are very similar countries, so very similar-looking people, from the same part of Northern Europe." But sensing that Kate is not getting any of this, I feel the need to explain further. So I do.

"I mean, I could've said Australian. I could've said Brazilian. I even could've said German. But that wouldn't have made any sense, would it Kate?"

"Why not?" she asks.

With yet more laughter and a rising sense of frustration in the room, I go on.

"Ok Kate, I'll tell you what. I will tell you the joke a slightly different way, and then I think you will understand, are you okay with that, Kate?"

"Uh-huh"

"So, we are in the water, remember that? Right? Then this fin comes up out of the water and starts moving towards us very quickly. We start to panic because we can't get back to the beach in time. But as this fin gets closer and closer and closer, we realise that it's not a fin.....it's a Nigerian!"

I go on... "You see, that wouldn't work now, would it Kate?"

Even more perplexity from Kate, "Why not?!"

Blimey O'Reilly!

"Because Kate, Finnish people from Finland in northern Europe tend to be very pale-skinned with straight hair. Whereas people from Nigeria, in Africa, tend to be typically dark-skinned with Afro hair! It's all about mistaking a person from one country with a person from another country. Mistaken identity. I would never mistake a Finnish person for a Nigerian, would I? That's pretty much the joke!"

But much to everybody's hilarity juxtaposed with their amused frustration, Kate is still looking at me completely baffled by what I've just explained.

And then she says...

"Well... what happened to the shark?!"

Now I'm staring at Kate completely perplexed as the audience erupts into raucous laughter. "Kate! There IS no shark!" I tell her!

"But... you said there was a shark!" she barks back.

"No, I didn't!"

Kate is having none of it! "YES, YOU DID!"

God bless poor bogan Kate and her simple ways.

"Kate. I'm going to explain to you how jokes work, okay? Now, comedy in many ways, is like magic with words. You know how when you watch a magician on stage, right? And they make something disappear?"

"Yes..."

"Ok, well it doesn't really disappear. The magician, or illusionist, just makes you think it's disappeared. It's called 'misdirection', Kate. Something disappears, and then something different appears. That doesn't actually happen, the audience are just made to think it does, or believe, that it's happened. That's misdirection."

"In comedy, we do a similar thing. I say a 'Finn' is in the water, and especially because it's Australia, people think shark. Because sharks have fins on their backs."

Kate says, "WHAT?!"

"No Kate, I don't mean that sharks have Finnish people on their backs! They don't surf sharks in Finland. That would be weird. They have fins for swimming and balance..."

"But I don't mean a shark at all. I mean a Finnish person, from Finland!

Misdirection. And like double misdirection, because what I actually mean is not a Finnish person at all, but a person from Norway!"

Then Kate tilts her head like something had dawned upon her and after a brief moment of contemplation says, "I still don't get why it has to be a Norwegian!"

Give me strength!

"Because Kate, Finland and Norway are both Northern European, Scandinavian countries!!!!

Then, amid all the laughter at Kate's simple yet adorably frustrating questions, a bloke at the back puts his hand up and exclaims, "Er, mate, I think you'll find that Finland isn't actually regarded as a Scandinavian country!"

For fuck's sake! It's just a shit joke, man! Can I go home now!!!

You see how scary stand-up comedy can be?!

There is no me!

Chapter 24 - Finnished

Rather ironically with regard to, and to follow on from, my earlier tale of watery scariness, much like some shark species and their swimming habits, the story just goes on and on and on.

It should be qualified however, that the fact sharks must keep swimming or they will drown and die is actually a bit of a myth. Whilst that may be true for a few species of shark, such as the infamous great white featured in Steven Spielberg's 1975 classic 'Jaws', which uses 'obligate ram ventilation' to breathe, which means it must constantly swim to survive to push water through their gills, most sharks use a method known as 'buccal pumping', which is basically cheek muscles pumping water through. Like bogan Kate, if you're not laughing, you're learning.

"Thank the Lord for buccal pumping. Now, what's on Discovery?"

So there, most sharks can in fact be like comedians and just laze around for hours doing fuck all and going nowhere.

The first example of this constantly moving, evolving and developing story was at the Melbourne International Comedy Festival, right after the first story with Tyler and Kate took place in Adelaide. Of course it is customary to make fun of Adelaideans when in Melbourne (and vice versa when in Adelaide. That's right, you both get 'paid out') and as such I told the Melburnians the story of the simple bogans in their rival city the month previous.

Of course, they were highly amused by the story of their undesirable South Australian brethren in 'Radelaide' and the deconstruction of said joke, which did give me the idea that there could be a show based around such stories.

Then, after the show had finished and the queue to leave died down, I was approached by a lady - I would say in her early 50's - who informed me that, "I am from Finland!" I enquired as to why she didn't tell me this whilst I was on stage. She replied, "I didn't want to interrupt and ruin the flow of the show."
How very German of her.

She went on, "I should let you know though, that in Finland we have a rivalry with Sweden, not Norway. So maybe you should say Sweden in your joke."

I explained to her that, "Yep, I know that Finland does indeed have a rivalry with Sweden, not Norway and in fact, when I first thought of the joke, I was going to use Sweden. However, I felt Norway would work better within the context of the joke."

The Finnish lady was quizzical as to why, so I explained.

"Well, it's easier to say 'Norwegian' rather than 'a person from Sweden'."

"Ah, she replies, "But you could say, a Swede!' That's even shorter!"

"Perhaps," I responded, "But whilst that might be shorter, it doesn't quite roll off the tongue like Norwegian does. Nor-we-gian has a nice little flow, whereas 'a Swede' does not."

The Finnish lady looked a little bit confused, perhaps with my answer being a little bit contradictory along with the fact that there might be a problem with a slight language and com-munication barrier.

As such, I explained further why the use of the word 'Swede' doesn't work as well as 'Norwegian'.

"You know that a Swede is also the name of a vegetable?"

She nods.

"So you see, another thing which helps make people laugh at jokes, is the audience immediately understanding what you're talking about when you hit them with the punchline, rather than have to think too much about it. Hence the problem with Kate in Adelaide. She didn't at all understand that I was talking about a human being, rather than a shark."

The Finnish lady continued to listen, so I continued to explain.

"When I say Norwegian, the audience immediately under-stand that I didn't mean a shark at all, but in fact a person from Europe. If I say 'Swede', then a lot of people in the audience might say to themselves, 'Why is there a vegetable in the ocean?' or 'A swede doesn't look like a dorsal fin!'. 'It wouldn't even float that way'. Or, 'Why not a cabbage?'. 'Why not a parsnip?'. Then you see, I've got a whole new set of problems on my hands rather than somebody just not understanding that I'm not talking about a shark!".

"Ahhhhh", says the Finnish lady. And I think, 'Finally, she gets it!'

Then she kind of stares at me in a moment of what I feel is her getting what I am saying and replies, "Yes, but you see in Finland, we have a rivalry with Sweden, not Norway!"

Give me strength....

Chapter 25 - Kiwi Bogans

More recently, I have come to really like people not understanding jokes, and the joy I get out of explaining and deconstructing them.

There's an old saying in the comedy business that goes, "If you've got to explain it, it's not funny".

I suppose that may be true in and of the joke itself, but at the same time, there is much joy and laughter to be had from picking the joke apart whilst having a bit of banter with the person who hasn't got it.

Take this one for example. Often here in the UK, or over in Australia, as well as many other countries of course, I tell stories about bogans and chavs. Those kind of people are always good for a laugh after all. Often doing things that they probably shouldn't be, and that shouldn't be funny, but are hilarious nonetheless.

And when I say bogan I often have to explain the term. I do so by way of a bit of a joke at the expense of our Antipodean cousins.

"If you are not aware of the term 'bogan', in England we call them chavs. In Scotland they often call them NEDs, as in non-educated delinquents. In America, as everybody knows, they are called rednecks. In Australia, they are called bogans. In New Zealand, they call them….Australians!"

Oh, how we all love to laugh at the classless Australians.

So, anyway, I'm doing a show at the Melbourne International Comedy Festival and because there are many of these Aussie people in the room, I like to use my little bogan joke as an ice-breaker near the start of the show. Over the years, I have come to realise that the Brits and the Aussies do love a bit of piss-taking banter after all.

So, as I'm about to come to the final word in the punchline, which as I said earlier is, "In New Zealand, they call them.... Australians!" I hear a voice from just to the left of the stage shout out, "BOGANS!"

I turn my attention to the source of the voice, which is from one of two pretty ladies in their mid twenties sat right in the front row. I ask "What?" and one of them replies, "In New Zealand we call them bogans."

I ask her, "So, you're from New Zealand?" And they both reply at the same time, "That's right, we're Kiwis," in a very New Zealand accent. Or rather, a very 'Na Zilland iksunt'. One of them goes on, "...and in New Zealand, we call them bogans."

I said, "I know that."

"That's right, bogans," she repeats herself.

"Well, thing is," I say, "That wouldn't work as a joke, would it?"

"But that's what we call them," she continues.

"Ok," I say back, "Let's try the joke your way, shall we?" I start again. "So, in England we call them chavs, in America, as everybody knows, they call them rednecks. In Australia, they call them bogans. In New Zealand, they call them... bogans!"

"You see? That doesn't work does it?"

"But....that's what we call them."

"Yes," I reply. "I know that in New Zealand you call bogans 'bogans', and in some parts of your country, 'Westies'. But that's not going to work as a joke, is it?"

She stares at me confused, so I go on.

"Listen, I'm going to explain to you what makes a joke work. Firstly, jokes kind of have to have a twist in their punchline, a surprise if you like. You see, so if I say 'in New Zealand they call them bogans', that's not a twist is it? That's just a fact."

Still staring at me.

"Problem we really have here is, we are at the Melbourne International Comedy Festival, not the Melbourne International *Fact* Festival!"

Despite rising amusement and many titters in the audience, something appears to be going on in her head now. Maybe she is starting to get it, but I proceed all the same.

"Another thing about jokes, is they tend to have a premise. The premise on this occasion being that as a British person, it's my duty to look down on and take the piss out of our lower class 'bogan' Australian cousins."

The audience of said lower class Aussie cousins, are highly amused by my breaking down of what is a simple joke and more especially, the confusion on the woman's face, as I continue.

"But what I am also doing on this occasion, is using your home country of New Zealand to compound the fact that we all look down on the Australians. You know, because New Zealand is generally seen as a more intelligent and sophisticated, if much smaller, version of Australia."

She starts to smile.

"You see now however, what you've just done in front of 120 Australians sat here in this room in Melbourne, is prove that that's not fucking true, is it!"

Then a little smile comes over her face as she appears to contemplate all I have just said to her and says back to me in her funny little Na Zilland iksunt, "Yeah... but in New Zealand, we call them bogans."

Give me more strength...

Chapter 26 - Hung Like a Horse

Now, the more observant amongst you may have noticed, in these aforementioned tales, that with regard to the people questioning what, in my opinion, were pretty easy-to-understand jokes, they all happen to be... That's right, female.

What? Can it be true that women don't get jokes, like men do? Do men really have a much better sense of humour and understanding thereof? Hmmm, surely not. But given the evidence, surely that must be the case!

Ah, but let's look a little closer, shall we? Let's delve a little deeper in said battle of the sexes.

Over the years, I like to consider the fact that I, like a lot of stand-up comedians, have become almost amateur psychologists. In that I mean you learn to read a room. This may be based on other comedians that are on stage before you, watching people filter into their seats, or just picking up on the vibe of the audience.

And of course, when you are on stage you also become a bit like Daredevil (I loves a superhero reference, I does), in that your senses seem to become a lot more heightened. You are watching and listening out for all those little things you might have to deal with. You see and hear everything. Sometimes you even feel it, a bit like a Spidey Sense. (Yep, another superhero reference).

Picking up on all those little things that happen in front of you. Which is probably why comedians tend to get distracted and bothered by things that muggles in the audience probably don't notice.

Superpowers, as we know after all, are just as much a curse as a blessing.

For example, there was another time when I did my shark joke at the Adelaide Fringe and again, a woman visibly didn't get it and so leaned in and whispered to her boyfriend clearly to ask him to explain the joke. His response was to give her a gentle nudge and directed her eyes back towards paying attention to me on stage.

Most people would take that to mean he was saying to her that she shouldn't talk whilst a comedian is on stage. But to my super-powered heightened senses, I realised that what he actually did was deflect, because the truth of the matter was that he didn't get the joke either! Only difference was, he was too proud to admit it!

And therein lies the rub!

It is simply not the case that men get jokes better than women, or have a better sense of humour, it's just that women don't suffer from that foolish alpha male pride where they can't admit that they didn't understand a joke.

Although, that being said, I have been told on many occasions by both men and women, that men do tend to like more jokey jokes, whereas women tend to prefer funny stories. Reason perhaps being is that men like to leave a comedy club with jokes to impress their friends or work colleagues with the next day. Whereas women would much prefer to hear a story about a comedian's life and walk away feeling like they've had a tad more of a connection with that person.

Is that true? And if it is, is it something to do with society? How men and women have been brought up? Is it that big scary invisible (but all-too-present in every day life) thing 'the patriarchy' that is to blame? Who knows? Probably best leave that one to the professional 'proper' psychologists.

But either way, I think we can put the age-old mass debate about who is funnier - men or women, or male or female comedians - to bed. However, with the exception of hen parties (often much worse than stag parties), I think female audiences can be generally better, or more fun, than male ones.

There's none of this macho male bravado nonsense; they are happy to let go and laugh, and admit when they don't get something you said and run with it. It doesn't matter where the funny is coming from as such, as long as everybody in the room is having a good time. Some psychobabble like that anyway.

However, a little word to the wise with regards to men who bring female loved ones to live stand-up comedy shows…

Again, Melbourne Comedy Festival at our regular venue in the city centre, the Elephant and Wheelbarrow, programmed by our good friend Terry North… an English expat who lives on the outskirts of the city in the Dandenong Ranges.

We are doing a UK showcase and I am MC with the middle act being Stephanie Laing. Stephanie often walks the comedy line of unassuming surreal comedy juxtaposed with some good old-fashioned filth. Sweetly dirty effective stand-up in my humble opinion.

On this occasion her performance is no different, as her closing routine, which is based around the opinion from the audience as to whether she should have a threesome or not, poses a simple question about whether anybody in the audience has partaken in such an activity.

A young-ish Australian bloke puts his hand straight up the air and exclaims, "I've had a threesome!"

Stephanie asked him what happened and he told her that he and his mate and a woman friend got together this one time and the threesome ended spectacularly with him *"ejaculating on my mate's leg!"*

So, I went back on stage as MC after Steph's set and immediately focused my attention on 'Mr Ejaculate on his Friend's Leg'.

"Mate, I've never had a threesome. I'm unlikely to ever have a threesome. I don't even want a threesome," I inform him. "But even I know that's not how it's meant to end! With you cumming on your mate's leg!"

"I guess you're right," he says.

"I know I'm right!" I state. "And more importantly, why would you tell a hundred strangers in a room this ridiculous thing you did?"

He puts his head in his hands, "I know. I'm an idiot," he embarrassingly admits.

"Yes," I tell him. "You are!"

Next to him I noticed a rather attractive woman of a very similar age, so I ask, "Are you… his girlfriend?" She nods.

"Did you know about this threesome?" I proceed.

"Yeah, it happened before we started going out a couple of years ago. He told me a few months back," she replied.

So I turn back to him. "Why would you tell your girlfriend this story?!"

"I don't know!"

"Because you're a silly twat, that's why!"

"I know!" he accepts.

Now, given that it's my duty as a British comedian, I have to take the piss further. It's only right! So, back to the girlfriend!

"You appear to be genuinely really lovely. What are you doing with 'Mr Spunk On His Mate's Leg' here?" I ask. "Is it a big cock or loads of money."

She shakes and lowers her head slightly. "It's neither!"

Brilliant! Score one to the lady. Embarrassing her wally boyfriend to raucous laughter from the crowd. Banter ensues in which I have to make fun of his job worthlessness and tiny penis. Again, it's my duty.

Then his girlfriend goes on. "By the way, just so you know," she points to a woman at the end of the row of seats behind them, "You see that woman on the end there. That's his mum!"

The comedy gods are looking down on me tonight!

"Mate, did your mum know this story?!"

His head goes in his hands, "No, I forgot she was there!"

Of course, the Melburnian audience are loving this!

"So not only have you been stupid enough to tell a comedian this story, a room full of strangers and your girlfriend a few months back, now your mum knows!"

He continues to shake his head.

Then I notice a man of a similar age to his mum sat next to her, so I enquire as to whether he is the young man's dad.

"No," he replies in a deep, broad Aussie accent, "I'm the stepdad."

"I bet you are really proud of your stepson with the tiny willy!" I ask.

"Actually, everybody is making fun of my stepson," he says, "but I'm quite proud of him. He's a good lad and also, I happen to know he is hung like a horse."

I hope I'm not alone in thinking that it's weird a stepdad would know that about his stepson.

But before I can say anything the mum, who has said nothing up until this point chips in, "YEAH, A SEAHORSE!"

Superb! Score number two to the ladies!

So, firstly, never underestimate how funny women can be, especially in an audience.

And secondly, never, ever, ever, take your mum to a comedy show with you. She will embarrass you every time!

"What do you think this is?!"

Chapter 27 - Lurching Klaus

Of course, since we are talking terrible stereotypes with regards to people not having a sense of humour, Das Deutschlanders.

You see, I thought it was just a British thing, but it seems that the whole world believes that the Germans don't have a sense of humour. Yep, most Europeans, Americans, Canadians, Australians, New Zealanders and even throughout all of Asia, it seems.

I do wonder what exactly they've done for that stereotype to spread across the entire planet. Maybe a study will have to be carried out?

However, I would say given my experiences of doing many shows in the capital of Berlin, a few in Hamburg and a couple in Frankfurt and Leipzig, the Germans do have a sense of humour, it's just a bit weird.

For example, take the joke that I often use as an icebreaker at the Australian comedy shows. The one about the bogans. In order to give that joke some kind of relevance to the Teutons, the first ever time I did a gig in Berlin, I asked the audience what they call those kind of people in Germany.

"In England we call them chavs, in Australia they call them bogans, in America they call them rednecks," I inform the crowd. "What do you call those kind of people here in Germany?" I ask. And an older man in the front row replies, "We call them foreigners!"

There you go, a sense of humour is there somewhere.

But it doesn't stop there.

Years later, after many more shows in Deutschland and a few more gigs throughout the summer following my shark joke deconstruction stories, I soon find myself back at Cosmic Comedy in Berlin.

And given that my Brummie expat matey Dharmander, who comperes the show, likes a bit of shark joke deconstruction, I give it another run out. Or swim out, if you'd prefer a bit of shark-based bad punnery.

From the look on his face, a young, tall lanky Aryan-looking German bloke didn't get the joke either. All his mates laugh, but he doesn't. So me and his mateys, who are from various places around Europe and the world join me in mocking their friend, who can't quite get the simple joke.

One of his mates happened to be Australian, with lots of dark hair and mutton chops. He looked like a chubby Wolverine and I was never going to let that go, so he got the piss taken out of him too.

I mean, Klaus is from a European country, so unlike Kate who lives in Australia, he has no excuse really.

At every opportunity, meself, his friends and a few other people in the audience give Klaus a bit of a ribbing about him not understanding my joke, and to be fair to Klaus, he sits there and takes it well, like the good German boy he is. He did look very German too. He was just missing the lederhosen and the cap with a feather.

But then after the show, I do a bit of what some comedians - and more especially Matt Price - call 'vicaring' at the door on the way out. Vicaring is basically shaking hands and thanking the audience for coming to the show, a bit like a vicar would do as people leave his congregation.

One of the last people to come to shake my hand was the tall German boy, Klaus.

I see him slowly walking towards me like a young version of Lurch from the Addams Family, and as he puts his long, skinny arm out to shake my hand, a wry smile comes over his face and he says to me, "So, the shark was Norwegian?"

Fucker! He got it all along! HE was playing US!

"You bastard!" I said to him. Then he laughed and walked off.

You see, the Germans do have a sense of humour. It's just a bit weird. And Klaus was no exception.

I should add however, that I never actually asked him his name. I just decided to give him a stereotypical German name. I think that's allowed. Although, I did look up the name Klaus and it turns out it's actually like a German version of my name Nicholas.

Hence the name 'Santa Claus'. Saint Nicholas.

Again, if we are not laughing, we are learning, people. This book is turning into more of an education than comedy.

Chapter 28 - UFC or KFC

Now, relationships, yes, they can and will often be an issue when you do this 'job'.

I say 'job', because many people including friends and family don't view it as a "proper job". That can be problematic in some ways too, but that's for another time.

If it's not the fact that one will be working until at least 11pm or midnight with most gigs, one tends to be away most weekends as well. And if, like me, you do the so-called 'festival circuit', it can be weeks you are away. Months on some occasions, like with the Australian comedy festivals in Perth, Adelaide and Melbourne which are all back-to-back from late January up until late April.

And of course, on that most romantic of all days, Valentine's, I'm always attending the Adelaide Fringe in South Australia.

Still, as we all know and have faith in, love can come in many different forms and many different locations.

A few years back on said day of love, after a late show at a venue myself and Alex Petty were running as part of our Laughing Panda 'empire' called the Belgian Beer Café just off Rundle Street on Ebeneezer Place, meself, a couple of the acts and the audience - being the lonely loveless dogs that we were at the time - decided to go to for a few sherbets at pub called The Austral.

The Austral is a couple of minutes walk away and another venue we were programming at the time. It's a vibrant rough-

and-ready place, but fun, if rather loud, and they do jugs of beer at the very reasonable price of $11 for the performers there.

I have to confess to guzzling down many of those jugs myself over the years.

Obviously pouring the beer into a glass first. I'm not a complete savage.

We all sat down at a table outside... we had to... It's the law! Because bizarrely, Australian bars have an intriguing licensing law that if you have a drink outside you must be seated. I guess Australians can't be trusted to stand up and drink beer without punching each other in the head.

Mind you, the Austral isn't known for its unassuming and serene clientele, so it's probably for the best. Bogans after all, are known to frequent this establishment on a regular basis. And that was certainly the case on this particular occasion.

So, I'm sat there with the group of singletons and out of the corner of my eye I spy a shifty looking bogan in a dirty Adidas tracksuit top staggering around, and worse still, staring in my direction. I turned away so as not to catch his attention, since it's bad enough being single and lonely on Valentine's night, let alone getting into a drunken conversation with a wobbling madman. But then he approached me and shouts, "Mate! Mate!"

Obviously, I can no longer ignore said shady character, so looked in his direction.

Then completely unexpectedly, he exclaims, "I love you mate. I fuckin' love you. You're the best!"

I feel a sudden tinge of guilt. There's me judging this bogan as a bit of an annoying scumbag, thinking he's going to cause trouble or talk a load of shit at me, and all he wants to do is tell me that he loves me. Odd, but I'll take it.

"I've seen you loads of times mate and I think you are awesome!", he goes on.

Now, the Adelaide Fringe, whilst being the second biggest comedy fringe in the world, is in a city which is not much more than a large town really. As such, I do tend to get recognised there more than most other places. It's the part of the world that I would say I'm most 'famous'. More by virtue of the fact that I do shit loads of shows in a relatively small city. Sometimes seven over a weekend day like Saturday or Sunday and often four or five some week days. And being on the darker side of the skin tones, wearing baseballs caps and brightly coloured T-shirts, I'm not that easy to forget.

Therefore, it was safe to assume that the bloke stood before me had been to a few of my shows in the past, but it is still rare that anybody will tell me they love me in quite this way. As such, I'm virtually reaching for a pen to sign an autograph when he follows on…

"ANDERSON SILVA! I've seen all your fights! You're the best ever!"

Crestfallen.

But more to the point, in my head, I'm thinking, "Who the fuck is Anderson Silva?!"

So I replied, totally disheartened that this man was not a fan of my comedy, "I'm not Anderson Silva."

"Come on mate, I've been a fan for years. I know Anderson Silva when I see him!"

To put this ridiculous conversation to bed, I reached for one of my show flyers which happened to be on the table at our venue, and as I do, I informed him that, "I'm doing a show at the Fringe."

But rather than look at the flyer he holds his head in surprise and amazement, "ANDERSON SILVA IS DOING A SHOW AT THE ADELAIDE FRINGE?!"

"No! He's not! Because I'm not Anderson Silva!"I went on.

But the bogan isn't having any of it. And I still don't know who the hell he's talking about.

Then he says, "Mate, I love you and you're awesome, but..." and he raises his fists as he proceeds to tell me, "...I've always wanted to try and knock out a UFC fighter! And Anderson Silva! Come on mate. Let's have a fight! I'll give you 50 bucks for the chance to try and knock you out!"

Baffled by such a bizarre proposition, still looking confused and certainly not wanting to fight this bogan - or anybody for that matter - and especially not on Valentine's night, I decline his generous offer. But given this unsavoury, unusual and ridiculous situation, we still have Google on hand. So somebody at the table showed me on their iPhone who Anderson Silva is, and I took a quick look whilst the foolish bogan is prancing around like Muhammad Ali wanting to sting me like a bee.

Indeed, it turns out that Anderson Silva is one of the greatest UFC fighters in history. However, a cursory look through Wikipedia reveals that he is Brazilian. He speaks Portuguese and not English. Surely a huge fan would know this? So the clue, you dickhead bogan, is me having a conversation with you in English!

And fucking hell mate, whilst I have no hair like this Anderson Silva bloke (how he knows this given the baseball cap I am wearing at the time, I don't know) and I have a dark complexion like the South American, being one of the greatest mixed martial art fighters of all time, you couldn't find many fitter blokes if you tried.

He is UFC, I'm more KFC!

Also, this man must be absolutely minted. So why would he take 50 Australian dollars, which equates to about 140 Brazilian Real, for a street fight with a dirty bogan?

That's right, he wouldn't. However, I am not Anderson Silva, one of the greatest MMA fighters of all time who's probably worth a few million Reals. I'm Nik Coppin, a London-based UK comedian who travels around the world hoping to make a few quid at comedy shows. And I can assure you, when you've paid out thousands of pounds weeks and weeks in advance and won't see most of that back for more weeks until the festivals pay out the ticket money, I am not exactly flush.

So I thought, "Fuck it, he's a lot smaller than me and that's about five more jugs of beer at the Austral!

Anderson Silva in action! (Not me, obviously)

Chapter 29 - Miracle Dolphin

A good few years ago, I popped into a gig called Ivan's Comedy Gaff.

Ivan being Ivan Steward. A man in his early sixties that many felt was one of those people who was a comedy genius, but didn't seem to realise it himself.

When I first saw him he was doing this character called 'The Comedy Ref'. Absolutely hilarious stuff that always had me in tears of laughter. I wish I could describe the act properly, but it was essentially a tall skinny bloke in his sixties dressed as a football referee charging all over the place saying silly things and giving the audience red cards for 'misbehaviour'.

Hard to describe, but side-splittingly funny. Even funnier when members of the audience didn't get it and looked totally

bemused. The thing was, I don't think you were meant to 'get it'. It just was.

He went on to doing 'The Comedy Traffic Warden', which whilst still funny, could not match the high standards of The Comedy Ref. I think he used his 'Comedy Gaff' to try out this character and other material.

It was primarily a new material show, after all, being in a small room above The Wheatsheaf pub on Rathbone Place, by Tottenham Court Road station. The room could hold no more than 40 people comfortably and I regularly popped in for jollies and to throw out the odd new bit.

I watched Russell Brand there once doing some new material. He was a rising comedy star then, before he got as famous as he did and shacked up with Katy Perry. The next time I saw Mr Brand actually, he was hosting a thing called 'Kings of Comedy'. That was a kind of reality TV show similar to Big Brother where a load of comedians were locked in a house and had to do comedy challenges. We weren't part of the main show, but rather doing a 'pilot' version. Which wasn't even a pilot because it never went to air, it was just a dry run with newer acts to iron out the creases for when the bigger boys and girls stepped up the following weekend.
There were eight of us in this studio-built house in Bristol.

It was interesting, but I found it all a bit boring to be honest. I just wanted to have a laugh and drink red wine, but we had to do these comedy tasks that weren't funny at the best of times.

The main show lasted one season, which says all you need to know really.

I do remember the energetic overbearing Russell saying something quite ridiculous at one point. It was something to do with a klaxon going off to end one of the comedians sets in front of a live studio audience. The comedian said it wasn't five minutes, but only four minutes and thirty seconds according to his watch.

Russell came back with something like, "You are questioning the might of the huge Endemol International TV company by looking at your little Timex watch?!" The comedian didn't really have the wit to respond, but I remember thinking at the time, "Well, er, yeah mate. I am. Endemol make TV shows, Timex make watches which tell the time!" Of course, it wasn't my place to say anything, if the other guy was too overwhelmed and witless to come back with anything.

However, despite some of his quite public bad behaviours, I always found Russell Brand to be a nice enough bloke really. I remember a couple of years after that Kings of Comedy thing, I bumped into him on Wardour Street in the West End of London and he remembered me and said hello as I passed him, so he's okay by me. I'm sure he'd be pleased to know that too.

There was a similar thing a few years later called 'Show Me The Funny' and that was equally as dull and lasted one series. I remember The Scotsman's most infamous reviewer, Kate Copstick, who was one of the judges on that show saying to me how dreadful she thought it was when she came to my Edinburgh Fringe show.

Kate had a reputation of being a proper hard-nosed no-nonsense reviewer who I'd seen for years passing me by in Edinburgh and she always looked stern as fuck, so when she came to the Meadow Bar to watch 'Shaggers' the first year we did it at the Fringe in Edinburgh in 2008, I was a little bit nervous. That was back when I was a lot newer and really worried about what a reviewer thought and wrote. I don't really give too much of a shit now. A review, whether it be good or bad, is just one person's opinion. The relationship between you and the audience is what really matters.

It didn't help that it was probably the toughest show we had in that inaugural Shaggers run, but the closing act, Bethany Black ripped it up and saved the show. I got talking to Kate over a drink after the show and she turned out to be absolutely lovely. No-nonsense, but lovely. And in the hour or two I chatted to her, I came to learn how and why she thought of certain shows and acts the way she did. She just didn't like pretenders. It didn't matter if you were good or bad, but be genuine.

And I find her to always be genuine. So I was delighted when she rocked up at the first Edinburgh Fringe run of the kids show *Huggers*, as well as my solo show that same year, 'Caricatures' at the City Cafe. The latter being a show that juxtaposes comedy stories and drawings (sounds familiar) that I might resurrect at some stage. It can be ever-changing and fun. So I says to Kate when she turns up having just done the 'Show Me The Funny'

show on the box, "Hey superstar!"
and I loved her reply. "Oh fuck off!"
then followed it up by saying, "Show
Me The Funny? That show did everything but show you the bloody
funny!"

A serious but funny woman indeed
and she was more than fair with her
reviews of all three of the aforementioned shows. They weren't great
reviews, but good and fair. That's all
you can ask for really. I've heard that Kate is also into some
rather provocative and racy sexual stuff too, so that probably
helped her to like Shaggers. Saucy minx!

She's welcome at my shows anytime though, as I am sure she
would tell me if they were shit. And of course we'd laugh about
it. I hope.

So, anyway, I'd got a couple of new jokes I wanted to try out
at this show and one in particular. I was working on stuff about
animals and I've always quite liked dolphins, so had a few ideas
with regards to stuff based around those ever-smiling aquatic
mammals that aren't always the nice guys people think they are.

I do recall a very odd exchange I had once based around said
cetaceans and their sometimes less than desirable behaviour.
You see, back in my younger days I had an earring which had a
dolphin bracelet charm which I put on it. I was at a Mirth
Control Comedy Christmas party at the Porcupine pub near

Leicester Square and got talking to a woman who was a friend of the organiser's wife. I don't like to be mean, but you could see she was a bit tapped in the head. Mad drunk and saying all sorts of silliness, but amusing nonetheless.

She asked about the little 9-carat gold dolphin on my earring and I said that I have it because I quite like dolphins. I then went on to impart some dolphin knowledge in that people think sharks are the always bad guys and dolphins are always the good guys. But as we should all know by now, despite movies like Jaws and their sequels, where great white sharks swim to the Bahamas to seek revenge on American families, sharks can be quite social and only tend to attack humans more because of mistaken identity.

Whereas dolphins, being the highly intelligent creatures that they are, have often been known to go about in gangs and beat up weaker dolphins, rape female dolphins and even commit infanticide because female dolphins stop having sexual inter-course to raise their children.

Then all of a sudden, this woman exclaims, "So, you think rape is a good thing?!"

I was like, "WHAT?!" I mean, how did she come to such a conclusion?!

She went on, "Well you said dolphins rape other dolphins! And you like dolphins, therefore you think rape is a good thing!"

Jesus H. Christ! Much like a dolphin in SeaWorld jumping to nose poke a giant beachball, that is one hell of a leap! Some people have some twisted shit going on in their brains, man!

I mean, human beings sometimes rape and murder other human beings and I like human beings, but that doesn't mean I'm an advocate of such heinous crimes. Blimey O'Reilly.

So, my bit of material. Here's what happened.

I said on stage, "You know sharks tails move side-to-side when they swim, whereas dolphins and whales tails move up and down?", as I did the motions with my hands. "Well, marine biologists and scientists will often say that the tail of a dolphin is the perfect swimming tool crafted over years and years of evolution by Mother Nature. I'm like, nah, it's just a fluke."

As I delivered the punchline, the entire 15-strong audience on a Wednesday night all laughed out loud at my brand new bit! Brilliant, I thought!

Then I went on to say, "Great! So you all know that a dolphin's tail is also sometimes known as a 'fluke'?" and they all shook their heads in confusion.

I went on to say, "Yes, they're called 'flukes'!"

More head-shaking from a confused audience.

So, I went on to ask, "So, if you didn't know that a dolphin's tail is called a fluke, why did you laugh at the joke?"

And at least half of the audience in slightly different ways, all said, "We don't know, we just thought it was funny."

Yep, everyone in the audience laughed out loud at a joke even though they didn't get the reference at all and had no idea what I was talking about! Mind. Blown.

Thinking about it now though, I like that joke. So I might have to re-introduce it, even if people don't get it. Un-realised genius. A bit like Ivan.

Chapter 30 - Guilty Purchase

Myself and fellow mixed racer comedian and kids entertainer Mike Belgrave used to enjoy some very nice lunch/dinner and beer get-togethers.

As well as many other piss-ups, of course.

Sadly for the circuit, but probably good for him, he stopped all this comedy shenanigry and is now a full-time teacher after having two lovely kids.

But I do remember one time in particular, before his wife Sophia popped out their sprogs and they still lived in delightful Peckham in South London, when I went round for a little lunch soirée with Mikey.

One of the few good things about Mr Belgrave is he always loves to cook. And none of this nouveau cuisine or vegan/vegetarian shite, no! Sausages, chicken and burgers are the usual order of the day, and lots of them! And more!

Top man.

As such, given his culinary loveliness as well as having some booze already in the flat, my instructions were to just "bring a few beers". Lovely, I can do that.

And rather conveniently, there is a Morrison's two minutes around the corner from where he lived. So in I go and head straight for the alcohol section. I love a bit of laser-guided shopping, me! You go in, you get what you want, you get out. Classic smash and grab. None of that faffing around business.

So I head to the checkout with four large bottles of Tiger beer and put them on the conveyor belt.

No sooner have the bottles hit the belt and I've reached for the 'next customer please' thing, when this old lady in front of me starts looking at me. Not necessarily a lingering look, but a look that makes one feel that she's thinking something. Whatever it is. Especially when she then looks at the four large bottles of Tiger. And then back at me. And then back at the Tiger. And then back at me.

Then she says, "Is that all you're getting, young man?"

She looked like an older version of my Aunt Rita so I'm sure if I were lighter-skinned I would've blushed with the slight embarrassment I was feeling.

"Er.....yes...."

She continued to look at me and the bottles of Tiger, so I continued.

"You know, like, I don't always just buy alcohol. I would normally buy food and other stuff as well, but I'm going to lunch at my friends house and he already has food so this is all I need to get..."

I thought to myself that's a good enough explanation, but there is still this look on her face, so I've hardly had time time to draw breath and so feel the need to further explain myself.

"It was what he said. His idea. Just get beers he told me. No need for anything else..." I ramble on. She still has this look on her face and I'm starting to feel like maybe I should go back and get some food so she doesn't think I'm some kind of raging alcoholic.

Then she says - as her face changes from one of my assumed judgement to one of confusion - "It's just that I have loads of shopping here, so if you're only buying those beers, I thought I'd ask if you wanted to go in front of me."

Oh… er, no… I'm fine…

Mike 'Biffa' Belgrave

Chapter 31 - Roper Dope

The Rope-a-Dope is the amazing tactic that Muhammad Ali implemented to bring down George Foreman in the 7th round of the Rumble in the Jungle. This is not to be confused with Andrew Roper... dope.

Roper is a tall scraggy-haired Australian who lives on the Gold Coast. Yes, he was a UK resident for about 10 years I believe, before his better half got a great job at university on the east coast of Australia and he had to go back.

That's right, man was told what to do by his missus, innit? He knows who's boss alright.

Still, I think he is one of the few Australians and expats that openly admits that he preferred living in the UK. Many of the Aussies who get booted out when their visas expire, and especially the expats, seem to be trying to convince you of something they don't believe themselves. Actually, they are more probably trying to convince themselves.

"Thank God my great grandad stole a loaf of bread and look where I am now, in paradise" and all of that nonsense.

Don't get me wrong, Australia is an amazing country and I love visiting and performing shows there. But one man's paradise is another man's inland taipan that will kill you dead with its lethal venom. Spiders too. I don't like those. Did I mention I don't like those?

I managed to eventually go and visit Roper Dope on the Gold Coast last year; it's a nice place. Years ago, when I was still working on London Underground Limited

I remember sitting in a cinema and seeing an advert for the Gold Coast in Australia which featured dolphins leaping out of the water in SeaWorld, surfers surfing, beaches and sunshine and I remember thinking, "Man, I am never going to be able to afford to go to such a place," by virtue of the fact that I used to spend too much of my not-so-hard-earned wages on going out on the lash too often and having no savings. Certainly not enough for a trip to Australia.But there I was! On the Gold Coast, walking its beaches, drinking in its bars, swimming in the blue waters. I didn't go to SeaWorld though. Not after watching Blackfish.

But despite the sunshine and everything, it wasn't as amazing as the advert.

I had expected that I guess, especially having been to many other parts of Australia for many years. However, I hadn't expected to be viciously attacked by some beastly jellyfish.

A 'bluebottle' it was. No, you stupid Brits and people not from Australia, not that little fly that buzzes around the place annoying people, but rather the nasty venomous jellyfish creature that lurks around Australian waters making a thorough nuisance of itself. Apparently the wind blew a job lot in at that particular time of year, which is rare. Had I looked up and down the beach and seen a load of dead ones (they're better that way), I might not have gone in the sea. But I didn't see them and so there I was happily floating away and then got what felt like a hundred bee stings up my arm. I did a quick flick and this long skinny blue thing flew off my arm and out to sea.

Then Roper strolls down the beach, sees that I've been attacked and tells me that he's lived there for years and hasn't been stung once. That's comforting to know, you bastard. Clearly a racist jellyfish.

The fucker left lots of little blue barb things in all of the stings up my arm as well. Bloody painful it was, the little fucking shit bag. Fortunately, I'm hard mate, so I could take the pain. Lesser men would've crumbled and whinged about it in a book.

Roper would've probably cried like the pussy he is if it happened to him too. Instead he found it all very amusing.

When I first met Andrew Roper, he was this lanky Aussie bloke with short hair wearing a suit. Looking almost like a professional comedian. The irony. Then one day I picked him up near Neasden station for a gig up north somewhere, and this bloke dressed in a T-shirt and jeans with long surfer-like hair approached the car. It took me a few seconds to recognise him, but then I thought it's got to be a midlife crisis or something, I reckon.

A couple of trips in quick succession we did together and the second time he drove us up in his tiny red Fiat Panda. Not that I want to disrespect pandas of course, what with them being the Shaggers show logo, but it just wasn't the car you would imagine an old surfer Australian man trying to re-live his youth driving.

But I still reckon what they say about men having big cars means they have small penises is nonsense. Because despite driving a small car, I'm pretty sure Roper has a tiny willy as well.

Still, we pretty much talked about Marvel comics and superheroes the entire way to the gig, overnight and back from the gig. Interspersed with Roper moaning about life and comedy like the miserable old git he can be.

Of course, it is always amusing to hear somebody rant about all sorts of shit. We do get a lot more cynical in our old-age after all. Still, life, comedy, superheroes and even more recently politics is always very entertaining to discuss with Roper Dope.

We have also stayed together and done many shows together in Australia at the Perth Fringe, Adelaide Fringe, Melbourne International Comedy Festival and of course the Edinburgh Fringe.

In fact Roper gave me the opportunity to play the greatest superhero of all time. Yes I was Roper'd into being Spider-Man in his Superheroes For Kids Show. The highlight of the show was me leaping onstage in uncomfortably tight bulging spandex. This lead to my character being dubbed 'Fat Spider-Man'. Children can be cruel. But this nickname wasn't from the children. It came from the other comedians. Who are also children.

Actually, I didn't really mind my little bit of superhero celebrity. The kids loved my Spidey antics, but that meant that I had to have photos with nearly all of them after every show. Courtesy of Roper telling them that was fine. Bellend!

Fat Spider-Man waiting to go on stage.

It seems Andrew Roper was already preparing me for the 2020 pandemic two years ago... by isolating me in a dungeon with a face-mask and lots of bog roll.

This meant crouching down to kid level over and over, which was hell on the knees and certainly not the best thing to be doing after being up until 3:30am on red wine the night before.

After a couple of years of playing said role, finally Roper managed to get me a proper(ish) costume as opposed to just a mask and a Spider-Man top. Despite the costume upgrade the Amazing Spider-man still had to wear Nik Coppin's trademark red trainers because the suit didn't cover my feet.

The most amusing thing about that situation was when fellow act Jay Sodagar's two young daughters came to the show with their mum.

I had my photo taken with them afterwards and then saw them on the street later that day with their mum. "You were Spider-Man!" they shouted at me. I of course denied it. Spider-Man had a brand new full mask and costume, how could they possibly know it was me? Then one of the girls looked down and said," Red trainers."

Smart girls.

At least they didn't call me Fat Spider-Man!

Anyway, Roper Dope came into his own at the Edinburgh Fringe just gone. That would be August 2019 depending on when you happen to be reading this.

It was all because of Debs. Debs being Deborah Lennard. A new-ish comedian who had requested a spot at Shaggers at the Brighton Fringe in May.

Now I wouldn't want people to get the idea that I run a show called " Shaggers " so I can chat up female comedians that I like. But this became a genuine concern when I decided that I did in fact like her. Clearly I had to tread carefully in the so-called courting department for fear of being seen as one of those sleazy comedians/promoters that cracks onto female acts. So I was very cautious.

Luckily it all worked out, because Debs was fine with sleazy comedians who crack onto female acts. Who knew?

Anyway, I had seen Debs who lived in the wonderful city of Brighton (forget the 'and Hove' bit; who cares about that?) very regularly throughout June and July but then I had to disappear for the month long Edinburgh Fringe. So, I was obviously missing the new lady whilst doing all these shows.

Two weeks later I get a message from Roper asking where I was in-between the kids show *Huggers* and the *Battle of the Superheroes*. I was across the other side of Princes Street getting some grub and paying some money into the bank. You don't hear that too often during a festival, I can tell you.

He told me to get over to The Three Sisters venue because there was something he wanted to talk to me about. More moaning and groaning from the grumpy git, no doubt.

But when I got there, not only didn't he appear to have anything to talk about, he just disappeared. Odd. He then reappeared with Debs! What an absolute delight of surprise. Apparently the two of them had been conspiring to surprise me with her visiting the Edinburgh Fringe unbeknownst to myself. Right from the day I left Brighton! Sneaky bastards!

However, a truly marvellous moment in a busy, frenetic and often knackering Fringe Festival, it has to be said.

So there you go, despite being a man going through a midlife crisis who moans like and even looks like a bitter old woman, Andrew Roper turned out to be a bit of a hero. Like probably his favourite superhero, Iron Man.

Although Tony Stark can put the alcoholic beverages away like nothing else. One glass of red wine and Roper is virtually on the floor crying for his mummy. Typical of a bloke who drives a tiny Fiat Panda.

In many ways though, as well as this very pleasant surprise he put time and effort into what is a busy couple of weeks of Fringe. Over the years Roper Dope has actually been a bit like a big brother with his advice and companionship and co-hosting shows and stuff over the comedy years. What a totally lovely chap, I adore him so much. Such a lovely man. Love him.

Stop being silly now, I'm only saying that because I know he would hate me to ever talk about him that way, the crotchety old Aussie bastard!

See, pulled off my own little rope-a-dope there, didn't I? Had you all thinking I was being really nice and kind about Roper Dope there, but I wasn't. I was being a twat like always. I'm like the Muhammad Ali of the comedy world. Bloat like a fatSpider-Man, sting like a jellyfish.

"Genius, billionaire, playboy, philanthropist, tiny cock!"

Chapter 32 - Jellyfish

Well, that's almost enough yarns for now, I reckon, so I suppose I should start to wrap this shit up. Or wind it down…

…or whatever.

In the sunshine of Perth seems like an appropriate place to do so. And yes, that is the really sunny version in Western Australia, not the drab and dreary one up the M90 from Edinburgh in the middle of Scotland.

Fresh from a ferry ride across from Fremantle to Rottnest Island and back.

And what a jolly day that was indeed. We have done that trip before of course. It's a marvellous cycle around the island, stopping off at some amazing beaches, as well as to take selfies with those most happy-faced of all creatures, quokkas.

Rottenest Island's name being derived from the Dutch for 'rats nest', given the place is full of the furry little beings. They are cute rats mind.

All of this as well as being greeted to the island on our ferry by a pod of dolphins. Which was very nice of them indeed. How delightful.

This day off from shows trip being taken with Alex Petty, Zak 'LJ DA FUNK' Splijt and Donal Vaughan. The latter having just acquired the nickname 'Jellyfish' on the way to said trip.

Donal 'Jellyfish' Vaughan being a bespectacled pudgy Irish-man with a balding noggin and the look of a man you wouldn't want to be anywhere near your children. Now before you start

Donal the Jellyfish

giving me scheisser about body and appearance shaming, it should be noted that Donal quite happily makes those jokes about himself in his stand-up act.

In fact, I've never known anyone to consistently tell and accept those kind of jokes on a more than regular basis about looking like a paedophile and not just accept it, but almost revel in it. I think he loves the attention, personally.

Maybe it's because he actually hates children and would rather actually keep his distance, rather than the other way round, hanging about school playgrounds. All very ironic given he actually does a very successful children's show at festivals and theatres here in Australia and in the UK. Either way, he's fun and funny. Smart bloke, even though he's prone to the occasional hissy fit.

His kids show is called 'Science and Magic' and it's basically him doing all sorts of weird science experiments with household objects. One of his 'tricks' involves him dipping his hand into a bowl of water mixed with washing up liquid and deodorant spray, removing his hand, setting it on fire and his hand being completely fine afterwards, being protected by the gooey liquid. It's a nifty trick.

But funniest thing I saw him do with regard to this trick was a spot at a geeky showcase we ran during the Adelaide Fringe in 2019. It was an adult show, so not for kids, but he did that routine not realising the air-conditioning was on blowing cool air towards him on the ceiling just in front of the stage. As he set his hand alight, the air-conditioning blew the flames back in his face. Fortunately he didn't get burned, but the look of surprise on his sea jelly face was hilarious.

Oh, how we laughed. Well, I did anyway.

Actually, speaking of kids and school playgrounds and since I'm currently in Australia, that reminds me of the time I was walking down the road to Glenelg beach in Adelaide and went past a field at a primary school. All the kids were having fun and rolling around in the grass on the other side of the field, but there was this one girl stood under a tree by the fence all by herself, just staring out onto the street.

She was a little blonde girl about seven years old and as I walked past she said, "Hello Mr Man." I replied in kind. Without the "Mr Man" bit obviously. She went on, "What are you doing today?" I replied, "Going to the beach." She said that was nice and asked where I was from. "England," I replied. "Ok. Have a nice day, Mr Man," she said. So I bid her farewell and carried on walking.

I've got to be honest, it freaked me out a bit. She was sweet and all, but had an air of a future serial killer in the making, or perhaps the ghost of a child who'd died in a school fire. Creepy stuff, man.

Present day, on Rottnest Island, post-bike ride, it came up as to how Donal had just acquired the name jellyfish, the long and short being that basically Donal made some reference to my darker skin as we stood at some traffic lights near Perth railway station. Such a racist! In turn I remarked that his pale skin was like that of a jellyfish. When I told Zak this, he interjected that jellyfish don't have skin, but of course being the fastidious chap that I am, I Google'd this. And the first thing that came up said that they do!

A mass debate started up and then of course, like most conversations, it all turned a bit more sexual in nature and I was instructed to look up whether or not jellyfish have genitals! This was the first thing that came up on Google:

"It drifts around in the ocean until it's sucked up by a female jelly-fish... The sperm is gobbled up by a single opening in the female - an opening which functions as a mouth, an anus, a vagina, and any other specialised orifice you care to think about."

After reading that I don't think I need to tell you that no more reading was done. Just much banter about jellyfish porn. The details of which I can't really remember and probably wouldn't write down if I could.

Such childishness, I know.

Then it was downing drinks and one more attempt at some selfies with a quokka en route back to the ferry. A quokka who, like the rest of his kind was completely unfazed and not worried about humans wanting to take his photograph and often actually make a point of coming up to have a closer look and a sniff. Mostly trying to steal some food from your bag despite the fact you are not allowed to feed them.

However, this little guy had clearly had a full day of tourist interest and as such couldn't really give a shit that we were there, didn't want to play and just wanted to be left alone to sleep.

"Quok off I'm sleeping!"

Meself and Zak Splijt down some virus-free Corona on
Rottnest Island… ahead of searching for jellyfish porn.

Epilogue

Yes, this is the epilogue. The actual epilogue. That last one, as I explained, was a chapter entitled 'Epilogue'. Because the story was centred around the ' Epilogue Lounge' in Alice Springs.

Is it that hard to understand? Blimey, you lot are such hard work.

So, yes, this would be the end of my first journey into becoming an author. Referring to myself in such a way makes me chuckle. I mean I barely write jokes, let alone a book.

If I'm honest I don't like to describe myself as a comedian either, and I certainly would not to call myself 'funny'.

I mean, you know, I *am* funny, honestly, but externally, it's more for other people to decide whether or not I am, what with comedy being subjective and all of that psychological maternal elephant. Er, mumbo-jumbo. See? I thought that was funny.

Either way, I do hope this has been at least a bit of an amusing read and helped you to forget , if only for a short time, the craziness that is going on in the world nowadays and indeed even prior to the lockdown, has been for a while now.

And like Tony Stark's Iron Man armour, the next version of this book may well have a few upgrades. But you are the proud owner of what will always be the first edition of my first ever book. I bet neither of us thought that would ever happen.

Speaking of Marvel Studios. At the end of Captain America: Civil War, there was title card that said 'Spider-Man will return'.

And he did return. And so will I, with more stories of comedy shenanigry at home and abroad.

Until the next time....

Nik x

A bookstore manager said we shouldn't use this photo because it looks like some middle-aged twat dressed like a teenager having a cup of tea and a pastry round at his nan's...

...just can't see it myself.

Biography - Nik Coppin

Nik Coppin has been a stand-up comic for more than 20 years, performing all over the world and has developed an international cult following. He has performed many solo shows at the Edinburgh and Adelaide Fringe Festivals, New Zealand and Melbourne International Comedy Festivals, all over Australia and the inaugural Hollywood Fringe Festival in Los Angeles, all to critical acclaim.

Coppin has made himself into what could be described as a worldwide circuit comedian having performed in many European countries such as Germany, Spain, Ireland, Hungary, France, Denmark and Norway. He has also toured Southeast Asia numerous times doing shows in Singapore, Cambodia, Vietnam, Thailand, Hong Kong, Japan and The Philippines.

His confident, affable and energetic style of comedy is quick to build audience rapport, as he talks about subjects as wide-ranging as human nature, his experiences in The Antipodes, Europe and Asia, his extensive knowledge of wildlife, super-heroes, current affairs and his mixed-race up bringing in London. His mother is English and his father is from Barbados.

As well as becoming one of the most professional acts on the comedy circuit, his versatility has also made him a much sought after compere. He has the ability to adapt to a multitude of audiences and is skilful, observant and affable enough put them immediately at ease.

Nik is also the creator, producer and MC of the international and hugely popular hit show 'Shaggers' where comedians of all varieties and sexual orientations are encouraged to talk about their sexual exploits to hilarious effect. A themed stand-up comedy show which has experienced sell-out performances around the globe, also to critical acclaim.

A spin-off from this show is the family-friendly show 'Huggers', which has become extremely popular and loved at festivals in the UK and Australia and added yet another notch in Coppin's belt having entertained small children.

This book is Nik's first foray into writing.

Review Quotes

"Fast and funny...Sweetly, charmingly and wildly hilarious host Nik Coppin's comedy was effortless audience loved it...(4 stars)

Rip It Up, Adelaide Fringe 2014

"Nik Coppin's carefree comedy and happy-go-lucky nature are irresistible... His rapid-fire style works no matter what the audience.... I can't wait to learn more about the world from him"

The Pun, Melbourne International Comedy Festival 2012

"Incredibly likeable" - **The Advertiser, Adelaide Fringe 2016**

"He talks at 100mph and generates an irresistible atmosphere of good old-fashioned fun" - **Chortle.co.uk, Edinburgh Fringe Festival 2010**

"Fun and amazing" (4 stars) - **Melbourne Comedy Festival 2010**

"Could Nik Coppin be any more spectacular? Fast paced, witty, fun and amazing, all without any pretension. The guy you want to be seen at, seen with." (5 stars) **Shaggers show, Melbourne International Comedy Festival**

"Amazingly funny stories, wickedly clever insights and a sense of fun that will drag anyone in. Super funny, super fun and charisma up the wazoo, Nik's awesome! 9/10" **Melbourne International Festival**

"The banter is slick and engaging....He goes off on the sort of wild tangents beloved of messers Izzard and Noble...immensely likeable and refreshingly uncynical" - **Chortle.co.uk, Edinburgh Fringe 2008**

"A rapid fire non-stop act full of energy. His hour went so quick, his charming smile and easy manner had the audience eating out of his hand and wanting more. Go and see him" **9/10 Melbourne Comedy Festival**

"My Dad has seen Richard Pryor roll out back in the day, and another relative has told me tales of what it was like to see Lenny Bruce both before anyone knew he was as well as Bruce at his prime. I have always been so jealous of them for that. But now, because of what I saw of Coppin's uber-pro performance in Hollywood, I can brag at them as they have at me!" (5 stars)

Audience member Chortle post, Hollywood Fringe Festival 2010.

Editor's Note: *We would like to point out that Nik's cartoon character on the back cover was NOT deliberately placed as if defecating on the United States of America.* 💩 💩 💩

Their President seems to be doing that rather well on his own.

Lightning Source UK Ltd.
Milton Keynes UK
UKHW011603270421
382715UK00001B/6

9 781910 614143